Independent Schools
Examinations Board

MATHEMATICS QUESTIONS AT 11+ (YEAR 6)

Book A:
Number, Calculations, Problems

compiled by
David E Hanson

Independent Schools
Examinations Board

www.galorepark.co.uk

GALORE PARK

Published by ISEB Publications, an imprint of Galore Park Publishing
19/21 Sayers Lane, Tenterden, Kent TN30 6BW
www.galorepark.co.uk

Printed by Stephen Austin & Sons

ISBN: 978 1 907047 88 6

First published 2005, reprinted 2013

Details of other ISEB publications and examination papers, and Galore Park publications are available at www.galorepark.co.uk

CONTENTS OF BOOKS A AND B

The list of contents is based upon *The National Numeracy Strategy: Framework for teaching mathematics from reception to Year 6*, DfEE, March 1999. A few changes to the original DfEE order and wording have been made and the sections have been given numbers and letters for convenience.

BOOK A

STRAND 1: NUMBERS AND THE NUMBER SYSTEM

A **Properties of numbers:** understanding properties of numbers and number sequences, including negative numbers

B **Place value; ordering:** understanding place value; ordering numbers; reading and writing numbers

C **Estimation and approximation:** estimating and rounding

D **Fractions, decimals, percentages, ratio:** understanding fractions, decimals, percentages and their equivalence; ratio and proportion

STRAND 2: CALCULATIONS

A **Number operations:** understanding number operations; relationships between operations

B **Mental strategies:** developing mental calculation strategies, including deriving new facts from known facts

C **Written methods:** using written calculation (pencil and paper) methods

D **Calculator methods:** using a calculator

E **Checking results:** checking that results of calculations are reasonable

STRAND 3: SOLVING PROBLEMS

A **Decision making; strategies:** deciding which operation, which method (mental, mental with jottings, pencil and paper, calculator), which equipment

B **Reasoning about numbers or shapes:** working out numbers or shapes; number puzzles; making general statements

C **'Real life' mathematics:** solving problems involving numbers in context; 'real life', money, measures

BOOK B

STRAND 4: ALGEBRA (PRE-ALGEBRA)

A   **Equations and formulae:** forming simple equations; expressing relationships; solving simple equations; using inverses; finding equivalent forms; factorising numbers; understanding the commutative, associative and distributive laws

B   **Sequences and functions:** identifying number patterns

C   **Graphs:** drawing graphs; developing ideas of continuity

STRAND 5: SHAPE, SPACE AND MEASURES

A   **Measures:** using measures, including choosing units and reading scales; measurement of length, mass, capacity, perimeter, area, time

B   **Shape:** knowing the properties of 2-D and 3-D shapes, including symmetry

C   **Space:** understanding position, including co-ordinates; understanding direction, angle; movement

STRAND 6: HANDLING DATA

A   **Data handling:** collecting, presenting and interpreting data

B   **Probability:** understanding basic ideas of probability

INTRODUCTION

THE CURRICULUM AND THE EXAMINATION SYLLABUS

The mathematics curriculum and the examination syllabus are subject to relatively minor changes or emphases from time to time, whereas the body of mathematical skills and knowledge which teachers consider valuable seems to remain fairly constant.

For completeness, and to allow greater flexibility in the use of this material, some questions included here may be outside the syllabus currently examined, even though they are likely to be within the capability of the majority of pupils in most schools. It is left to teachers to select questions which they consider appropriate and, in any case, it is assumed that teachers will wish to differentiate according to pupil abilities. Capable pupils may benefit from 'stretching' the current examination syllabus.

The material is mostly at National Curriculum Level 4, with some of Level 5 but, for completeness, questions cover ideas met in all years up to and including Year 6.

The contents pages outline the way in which questions have been grouped. This closely follows the latest official publications by the DfEE. The strands are numbered and the subdivisions of the strands are lettered for easier reference. It should be noted that these numbers and letters are not official.

THE QUESTIONS

The majority of the questions come from the 11+ Common Entrance papers (January 1990 to January 1999) and, for these questions, the paper and original question number are generally indicated. The original mark distribution has been retained in all but a very few cases where some adjustment seemed sensible in the light of experience. A number of new questions have been written in order to provide extra practice. These have been given appropriate mark allocations for consistency. Some grading in difficulty has been undertaken. Inevitably some original questions involve several skills and these have either been split or have been placed wherever seemed most appropriate. Some rewording and redrawing has been undertaken for clarity and consistency.

USING THIS BOOK

The book has been designed for use by pupils, under the guidance of a teacher or parent, as a resource for practice of basic skills and recall of knowledge.

Revision notes and worked examples have generally not been included, since such material is available in existing publications. Answers to the questions are not included in this publication; a separate, comprehensive answer book is available.

CALCULATORS

It is assumed that calculators will not be used in answering the questions in this book. Questions involving calculators concentrate on interpreting the display.

STRAND 1: NUMBERS AND THE NUMBER SYSTEM

A   **Properties of numbers:** understanding properties of numbers and number sequences, including negative numbers

1.   (i)   Count the number of circles here.

Answer: ....   (1)

(ii)   How many circles would there be if there were five fewer?

Answer: ....   (1)

2.   This drawing shows woodlice in a choice chamber.

light   dark

(i)   How many woodlice have chosen to be in the dark side?

Answer: ....   (1)

(ii)   How many woodlice are there altogether?

Answer: ....   (1)

(iii)   How many more have chosen the dark side than the light side?

Answer: ....   (1)

1

3. (i) Here is part of a number track:

				27	28	29				

Write the numbers 24 and 33 in the correct boxes. (1)

(ii) Count backwards in sixes from 100

100, 94, 88, ..., ..., ..., ... (2)

4. Complete these statements using the words **odd** and **even**:

(i) An odd number plus an odd number is always an .... number.

(ii) An odd number minus an .... number is always an odd number.

(iii) An even number plus an .... number is always an odd number.

(iv) An odd number multiplied by an even number is always an .... number.

(v) An .... number times an .... number is always an odd number. (5)

5. Write **true** or **false** for these statements:

(i) Every even multiple of 3 is divisible by 6

Answer: .... (1)

(ii) All multiples of 4 are even.

Answer: .... (1)

(iii) Every number ending in 0 or 5 is divisible by 5

Answer: .... (1)

6. Ann and Ben are playing a game on a path with numbered flagstones. They both start on the flagstone marked START.

START	1	2	3	4	5	6	7	8	9	10	11	12	13	14	15	16

(i) Ann can leap over two flagstones so she lands first on 3

Write a letter **A** on all the flagstones she will land on. (2)

(ii) Ben has shorter legs! He can only leap over one flagstone.

Write a letter **B** on all the flagstones he will land on. (2)

(iii) Shade all the flagstones which have **A** and **B** on them.

What do you notice about these numbers?

Answer: ....

.... (2)

7. Here is a number grid:

1	2	3	4	5	6
7	8	9	10	11	12
13	14	15	16	17	18
19	20	21	22	23	24
25	26	27	28	29	30
31	32	33	34	35	36

(i) Shade in 5 and then every fifth number. (2)

(ii) Put a cross ✕ on 3 and then every third number. (2)

(iii) What can you say about the numbers which are shaded and have a cross?

Answer: ....

.... (2)

3

8. (i) Class 4A has 12 pupils.

They have been told to group themselves in threes round tables.

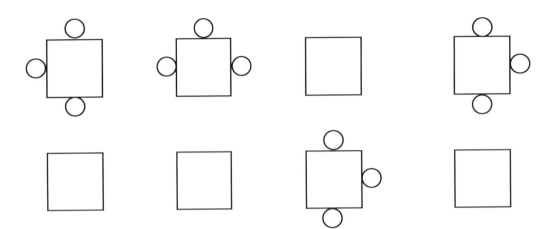

(a) How else could class 4A have been put into groups of equal size?

Answer: ....

....

.... (2)

(b) Suggest two other class sizes between 12 and 20 which could have been grouped in threes.

Answer: .... and .... (2)

(ii) Class 4B has 20 pupils.

With only 8 tables, how could they best be grouped?

Answer: ....

.... (2)

(iii) Class 4C has 17 pupils.

Why is it not possible to arrange this class in groups of equal size?

Answer: ....

.... (2)

4

9. Charlotte has been counting people entering the school hall to watch a play and has recorded a tally.

adults	ⅢⅢ ⅢⅢ ⅢⅢ ⅢⅢ ⅢⅢ ⅢⅢ ⅢⅢ ‖
children	ⅢⅢ ⅢⅢ ⅢⅢ ⅢⅢ ⅢⅢ ‖‖

(i) How many adults has she counted?

Answer: .... (1)

(ii) How many seats have been filled altogether?

Answer: .... (1)

10. Which of these numbers is divisible by 3?

16   36   42   98   102   301   1011

Answer: .... (2)

11. (i) In this list, circle the multiples of 4

8   14   20   28   30   42   48   52   60   (2)

(ii) In this list, circle the multiples of 7

14   27   35   42   54   56   63   77   91   (3)

12. (i) In this list, circle the factors of 48

2   3   4   5   6   7   8   9   10   11   12   (3)

(ii) In this list, circle the factors of 100

2   3   4   5   6   7   8   9   10   11   12   (2)

13. Here is a list of numbers:

              3   8   18   7   5   20

From the list, choose

(i) a multiple of 6

Answer: .... (1)

(ii) a factor of 10

Answer: .... (1)

November 96 Q4

14. (i) List all the factors of 12

Answer: .... (2)

(ii) List all the factors of 27

Answer: .... (2)

(iii) Which numbers are factors of both 12 and 27?

Answer: .... (1)

November 94 Q12

15. Write down six whole numbers which are factors of 30

Answer: .... (2)

January 93 Q3

16. 9 × 8 = 72 is a multiplication fact.
9 and 8 make a factor pair of 72
Find all the other factor pairs of 72

Answer: ....

.... (5)

January 92 Q12

17. Here is a multiplication square which has been partially completed:

X	1	2	3	4	5	6	7	8	9	10
1					5					
2		4								
3									27	
4										
5			15							
6			24		36					
7										
8							56			
9			27		54					
10										

(i) Carefully shade in the squares for all multiples of 9   (2)

(ii) Write all the square numbers in the correct places.   (3)

(iii) If the square were completed, how many times would 12 appear?

Answer: .... (2)

18. This Venn diagram shows multiples of 2 and multiples of 3

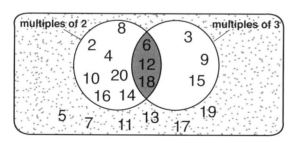

only the numbers from 2 to 20
are included in this study

(i) What can you say about the numbers in the shaded region?

Answer: .... (2)

(ii) What can you say about the numbers in the dotted region?

Answer: .... (2)

7

19. The numbers 2, 4, 8 and 16 form a pattern.

    Write the next two numbers in the pattern.

    Answer: .... (2)

    November 91 Q4

20. Draw the next square number.

    (2)

    January 91 Q7

21. (i) $5^2 = 25$

    What is 4^2?

    Answer: .... (2)

    (ii) $3^3 = 27$

    What is 2^3?

    Answer: .... (2)

    November 93 Q11

22. These drawings show models of cube numbers.

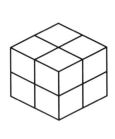 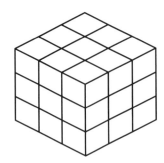 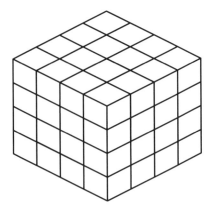

    Fill in the missing details.

    $2^3 = 8$ .... = ... = ... (2)

8

23. Study this arrangement of the counting numbers in order.

0	1	(2)	(3)	4	(5)
6	7	8	9	10	11
12	13	14	15	16	17
18	19	20	21	22	23
24	25	26	27	28	29
30	31	32	33	34	35
36	...	...	...	...	...
...	...	...	...	...	...

(i) What do you notice about the numbers in the left-hand column?

Answer: .... (2)

(ii) Complete the next two rows. (2)

(iii) Circle all the prime numbers. *(The first three have been done for you.)* (4)

(iv) What do you notice about the positions of the prime numbers except 2 and 3?

Answer: ....

.... (2)

(v) Amanda suggests that every prime number might be one more or one less than a multiple of 6

97 is a prime number.

Divide 97 by 6

What do you notice?

Answer: .... (2)

24. The first prime numbers are   2   3   5   7

Write the next eight prime numbers.

Answer: .... (4)

January 91 Q11

25. Circle the prime numbers in this list.

2   7   9   13   15   21   23   27   (2)

November 92 Q8

26. What are the next two prime numbers after 37?

Answer: .... (2)

November 90 Q7

27.   2   5   9   14   20

From the list of numbers above, write

(i)   a factor of 63

Answer: .... (1)

(ii)   a square number

Answer: .... (1)

(iii)   all the prime numbers

Answer: .... (2)

(iv)   the number which is a common multiple of 2 and 5

Answer: .... (1)

(v)   three numbers which add up to 31, using each number only once.

Answer: .... (2)

November 91 Q15

28. Here is a number sequence:

    4   8   12   16   20   24   28

Use one of these words to complete the sentences.

   prime   factor   square   multiple   cube

   (i)   Each number is a .... of 4.   (1)

   (ii) The numbers 4 and 16 are .... numbers.   (1)

   (iii) Each of the numbers 4, 8 and 12 is a .... of 24   (1)

   (iv) The number 8 is a .... number.   (1)

   November 98 Q2

29. Look at this list of numbers:

            2   15   9   48   8   3

   (You may use a number more than once.)
   From the list write

    (i)   a prime number

                                        Answer: .... (1)

    (ii) a square number

                                        Answer: .... (1)

    (iii) a factor of 24

                                        Answer: .... (1)

    (iv) a multiple of 4

                                        Answer: .... (1)

   November 97 Q6

11

30. Look at these numbers:

    10   36   21   8   7

    From the list, select

    (i)   a square number

                                    Answer: ....   (1)

    (ii)   a factor of 24

                                    Answer: ....   (1)

    (iii)   a multiple of 5

                                    Answer: ....   (1)

    (iv)   a prime number

                                    Answer: ....   (1)

    (v)   the product of 7 and 3

                                    Answer: ....   (1)

January 99 Q8

31. Here is a list of numbers:

    8   30   5   9   13   40

    From the list, write

    (i)   a square number

                                    Answer: ....   (1)

    (ii)   a multiple of 15

                                    Answer: ....   (1)

    (iii)   a factor of 20

                                    Answer: ....   (1)

January 96 Q5

32. Write the next number in these sequences.

    (i)   20   25   30   35   40   ....   (1)

    (ii) 27   33   39   45   51   ....   (1)

    (iii) 59   55   51   47   43   ....   (1)

    (iv) $^-47$ $^-36$ $^-25$ $^-14$ $^-3$ ....   (2)

33. Fill the gaps in these sequences.

    (i)   43   47   55   ....   (2)

    (ii) .... $^-3$ 3   6   ....   (2)

34. (i) Write the next two numbers in these sequences.

        (a) 81   64   49   ....   (2)

        (b) 1   3   7   15   ....   (2)

        (c) 1   3   2   4   3   5   ....   (2)

        (d) 1   2   3   5   8   13   ....   (2)

    (ii) (a) What sort of numbers are these?

            2   3   5   7   11

                  Answer: .... (2)

        (b) Give the next four numbers in this sequence.

            2   3   5   7   11   .... (2)

February 94 Q11

35. Give the next two terms in these sequences.

    (i)   4   7   10   13   ....   (2)

    (ii)   16   8   4   2   ....   (2)

    (iii) 1   3   9   27   ....   (2)

    (iv) 9   19   18   28   27   ....   (2)

November 93 Q13

36. Write the next two numbers in each of the following sequences.

    (i)   1   4   7   10   ....   (2)

    (ii)   1   2   4   8   ....   (2)

    (iii) 1000   100   10   1   ....   (2)

November 94 Q10

37. Write the next two numbers in each of these sequences.

    (i)   3   6   9   ....   (2)

    (ii)   108   96   84   72   ....   (2)

    (iii) 33   34   17   18   9   10   5   ....   (3)

January 97 Q3

38. Write the next two numbers in each of these sequences.

    (i)   1   2   5   10   17   ....   (2)

    (ii)   144   72   36   18   ....   (2)

    (iii) 4   10   9   15   14   20   19   ....   (2)

November 95 Q9

39. Write the next number in each of the following patterns.

   (i)   16   13   10   7   4   ....   (1)

   (ii) 1   2   4   7   11   ....   (1)

   (iii) 486   162   54   18   6   ....   (1)

   (iv) 2   2   4   6   10   ....   (2)

January 93 Q7

40. Continue these sequences of numbers.

   (i)   3   7   11   15   ....   (2)

   (ii) $\frac{1}{2}$ $\frac{2}{4}$ $\frac{3}{6}$ ....   (2)

   (iii) 1   4   9   16   ....   (2)

January 98 Q6

41. Continue these patterns of dots.

   (i)

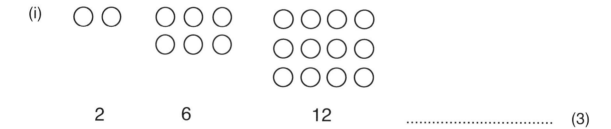

        2   6   12   ....   (3)

   (ii)

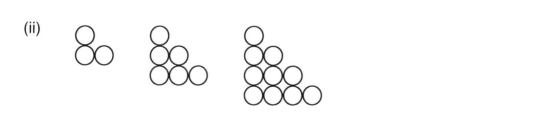

        3   6   10   ....   (3)

42. These two identical thermometers show the temperatures in °C inside and outside a window.

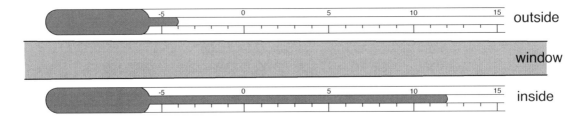

(i) What is the temperature inside the window?

Answer: ....°C   (1)

(ii) What is the temperature outside the window?

Answer: ....°C   (1)

(iii) How many degrees colder is it outside than inside?

Answer: .... degrees   (1)

43. Carol climbs a mountain.

When she sets off, the temperature is 12 °C but as she climbs, the temperature falls.

At the top of the mountain the temperature is 17 degrees lower than it was at the bottom.

What is the temperature at the top of the mountain?

Answer: ....°C   (2)

44. Basil is snorkelling.

He dives to ⁻5 m (five metres below the water surface) and looks at the underside of a shark 2.4 m above him.

At what depth is the shark swimming?

Answer: .... m   (2)

B **Place value; ordering:** understanding place value; ordering numbers; reading and writing numbers

1. (i) Which number is shown on this abacus?

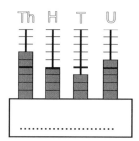

   (a) Write the number in figures.

   Answer: .... (1)

   (b) Write the number in words.

   Answer: .... (1)

   (ii) On this abacus, show 185

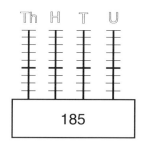

   (1)

2. Which number is shown here?

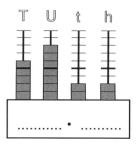

   (i) Write the number in figures.

   Answer: .... (1)

   (ii) Write the number in words.

   Answer: .... (2)

17

3. (i) On this abacus, show the number one hundred and five point zero four.

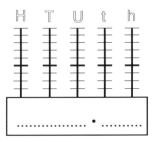

.... • ....

(2)

(ii) Write this number in figures.

Answer: .... (2)

4. (i) Write in numerals (figures) the number four hundred and twelve.

Answer: .... (1)

(ii) Write in words the number 194

Answer: .... (1)

5. Write in figures the number thirteen thousand and fourteen.

Answer: .... (2)

January 90 Q5

6. Write in figures the number twenty thousand three hundred and five.

Answer: .... (2)

November 91 Q1

7. Write in digits the number twenty thousand and thirteen.

Answer: .... (2)

January 93 Q1

18

8. (i) Which number is represented on abacus **A**?

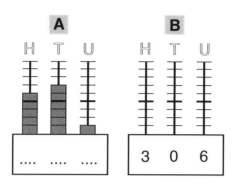

Answer: .... (1)

(ii) On abacus **B**, represent the number 306 (1)

(iii) Explain the difference between the 6 on abacus **A** and the 6 on abacus **B**.

Answer: ....

.... (2)

9. On abacus **D**, represent the number which is two more than the number on **C**.

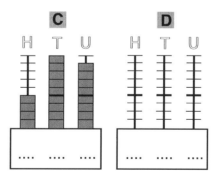

(2)

10. What is the value of the 9 in 109?

Example: the 6 in 3061 has the value 60 (6 tens).

Answer: .... (1)

11. (i) What is the value of the 7 in 3710?

Answer: .... (1)

(ii) What is the value of the 5 in 135 071?

Answer: .... (1)

12. What is the value of the number 3 in 1034?

Answer: .... (1)

January 91 Q2

13. (i) How many times more is the 6 on the H spike worth than the 6 on the U spike?

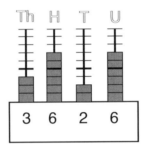

Answer: .... (1)

(ii) How many times more is the 4 on the T spike worth than the 4 on the h spike?

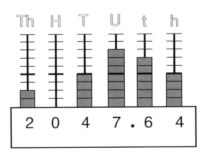

Answer: .... (2)

A B

14. In the number 163.62 how many times greater is the 6 marked **A** than the 6 marked **B**?

Answer: .... (2)

February 94 Q4

15. Put a decimal point in each of these numbers so that the 2 has the value of two tenths.

　　　　　3　1　2　　　　　　　6　2　0　　　　　7　9　2　3　　　　(3)

January 96 Q4

16. Look at this number:

2730

(i) What is the value of the digit 7?

　　　　　　　　　　　　　　　Answer: ....　(1)

(ii) 2730 is multiplied by 10

What is the value of the digit 7 in the new number?

　　　　　　　　　　　　　　　Answer: ....　(1)

(iii) 2730 is divided by 10

What is the value of the digit 7 in this new number?

　　　　　　　　　　　　　　　Answer: ....　(1)

November 98 Q1(a)

17. (i) Multiply 15 by 100

　　　　　　　　　　　　　　　Answer: ....　(1)

(ii) Divide 15 by 100

　　　　　　　　　　　　　　　Answer: ....　(1)

21

18. Abacus **A** shows the number 3510

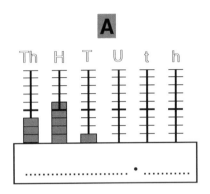
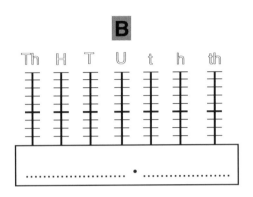

On abacus **B** show the number obtained when 3510 is divided by 1000 (2)

19. (i) Multiply 102 by 10

Answer: .... (1)

(ii) Divide 102 by 10

Answer: .... (1)

20. (i) How many times more than 420 is 420000?

Answer: .... (1)

(ii) How many times more than 30.7 is 3070?

Answer: .... (1)

21. Which of these numbers have a digit zero of the same value?

302   1060   30.5   0.58   3.05

Answer: .... (2)

22. Which two numbers have a digit 5 of the same value?

350   3502   3.5   5   156.3

Answer: .... (2)

January 92 Q7

22

23. (i) On this number line, the number 3 is shown as a black dot.

   Mark clearly with a cross (X) the number which is 7 less than 3   (1)

   (ii) On this number line, mark clearly the number ⁻2

   (1)

24. (i) Which number is shown on this number line?

   Answer: .... (1)

   (ii) On this number line, mark clearly with a cross the number ⁻3

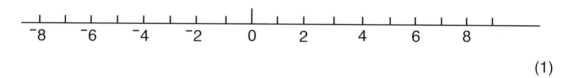

   (1)

25. (i) On this number line, mark clearly with a cross the number 0.8

   (ii) Which number is represented by the dot?

   Answer: .... (1)

26. On this number line, mark clearly with a cross the fraction $\frac{3}{4}$

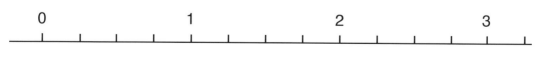

   (1)

27. (i) Give an example of a number between 35 and 45

Answer: .... (1)

(ii) Give an example of a number between 3.5 and 4.0

Answer: .... (1)

(iii) Give an example of a number between 0.4 and 0.5

Answer: .... (1)

28. (i) Give an example of a fraction between $\frac{1}{4}$ and $\frac{3}{4}$

Answer: .... (1)

(ii) Give an example of a fraction between $\frac{1}{2}$ and $\frac{3}{4}$

Answer: .... (2)

(iii) Give an example of a fraction between $\frac{1}{2}$ and $\frac{2}{3}$

Answer: .... (2)

29. (i) Which number is exactly half way between 8 and 18?

Answer: .... (1)

(ii) Which number is exactly half way between 38 and 52?

Answer: .... (2)

(iii) Which number is exactly half way between 64 and 128?

Answer: .... (2)

30. On the number line below, the number 3 is shown as a dot.

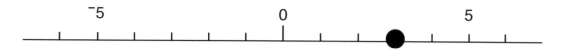

(i) Mark with crosses all integers (whole numbers) which are less than 3 (2)

(ii) Mark with circles all integers which are greater than 3 (1)

31. (i) On this number line, mark with squares all integers □ such that □ < 2

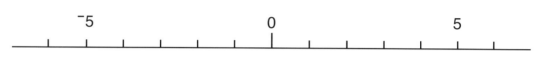

(2)

(ii) On the same number line, mark with triangles all integers △ such that △ ⩾ 3 (2)

32. On this number line, mark with circles all integers O such that ⁻4 < O < 6

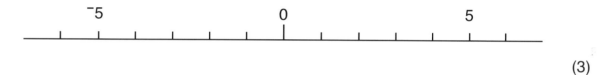

(3)

33. On this number line, mark with circles all integers O such that 11 ⩽ O ⩽ 18

(2)

25

34. Write these numbers in order of **increasing** size.

| 12 | 20 | 99 | 19 | 101 |

.... (2)

35. Write these numbers in order, the **smallest** first.

| 450 | 104 | 405 | 115 | 140 |

.... (2)

Specimen 94 Q1

36. Write these numbers in order of **decreasing** size.

| 3490 | 4039 | 943 | 3409 | 4309 | 3049 |

.... (2)

37. Put these numbers in order of size, starting with the **smallest**.

| 8.42 | 41 | 8.4 | 801 |

.... (2)

November 92 Q1

38. Put the following in order of size, starting with the **smallest**.

| 0.3 | 0.09 | 0.16 | 0.33 |

.... (2)

November 91 Q5

39. Write these numbers in order of **decreasing** size.

| 102 | 345 | 2001 | 1020 | 201 | 1200 |

.... (3)

40. Place these numbers in order, with the **smallest** first.

    3.1   29   3   2.9   31

    ....   (2)

February 94 Q1

41. Write these numbers in order of size, starting with the **smallest**.

    8.4   7.48   9.02   8.47   9.2

    ....   (2)

November 98 Q1(c)

42. Put these numbers in order of size, starting with the **smallest**.

    4.12   4.2   4   4.212   4.121

    ....   (2)

January 95 Q8

43. Put these fractions in order of **increasing** size.

    $\frac{1}{2}$ $\frac{2}{3}$ $\frac{1}{3}$ $\frac{3}{4}$ $\frac{1}{5}$

    ....   (2)

44. Put these numbers in order of **increasing** size.

    1020   1200   2120   1220   1022

    ....   (2)

45. Here are three boxes, **A**, **B** and **C**, containing sweets:

A	B	C
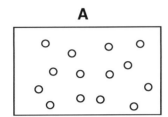	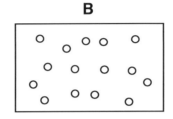	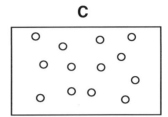

Write the letters in order of **increasing** numbers of sweets.

Answer:

.... (2)

46. Here are the times recorded in a 100-metres running race:

lane	1	2	3	4	5	6	7	8
name	Katie	Sophie	Robin	Keeba	John	Laura	Ruth	Oliver
time(s)	13.15	14.02	13.49	13.51	14.10	12.95	12.59	13.04

Complete this list of placings.

position	name	time(s)
1st	....	....
2nd	....	....
3rd	....	....
4th	....	....
5th	....	....
6th	....	....
7th	....	....
8th	....	....

(4)

C **Estimation and approximation:** estimating and rounding

1.

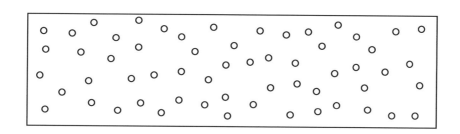

    (i)   Estimate (do not count) the number of circles in the rectangle.

                                       Answer: .... (2)

    (ii)   Now count the number of circles.

                                         Answer: .... (2)

    (iii)   How accurate was your estimate? Explain, or show, what you did.

          Answer: ....

          .... (2)

2.   (i)   Estimate the position of 2 on this number line. Mark it with a cross.

               ⁻5   0   5

                                                          (2)

    (ii)   Estimate the position of 45 on this number line. Mark it with a cross.

          0   200

                                                          (2)

    (iii)   Estimate the position of 800 on this number line. Mark it with a cross.

          0   1000

                                                          (2)

3. (i) Estimate (do not count) the number of dots in this rectangle.

Answer: .... (2)

    (ii) Explain how you did this.

Answer: ....

.... (2)

4. (i) Write 134 to the nearest ten.

Answer: .... (1)

    (ii) Write 451 to the nearest hundred.

Answer: .... (1)

    (iii) Write 2459 to the nearest thousand.

Answer: .... (1)

5. Write the number

273.6

    (i) to the nearest whole number

Answer: .... (1)

    (ii) to the nearest ten

Answer: .... (1)

    (iii) to the nearest hundred

Answer: .... (1)

6. Mary uses each of the digits 8 7 3 4 to make a four-digit number.

   Example: 4378

   (i) What is the smallest four-digit number she can make?

   Answer: .... (1)

   (ii) Write your answer to part (i) correct to the nearest 1000.

   Answer: .... (1)

   November 98 Q1(d)

7. When Jane multiplies 53 by 2.8 she gets an answer of 148.4
   Write this answer

   (i) correct to the nearest whole number

   Answer: .... (1)

   (ii) correct to the nearest 10

   Answer: .... (1)

   November 95 Q3

8. Which of the following numbers is nearest 2000?

             1495   2500   999

   Answer: .... (2)

   January 91 Q1

31

9. The crowd at a soccer match was recorded as 31 483

Write this to the nearest 1000.

Answer: .... (1)

10. The result shown by Amanda's calculator is

$$1\ 5\ 3\ 8\ 4$$

(i) Write this to the nearest 10.

Answer: .... (1)

(ii) Write this to the nearest 100.

Answer: .... (1)

11. (i)

lawn | vegetable patch

Estimate the proportion of this garden which is lawn.

Answer: .... (2)

(ii)

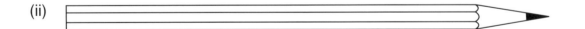

Tanya estimates that her pencil gets about one cm shorter every day.
Estimate the length of the pencil in five days' time.

Answer: .... cm (2)

12.   (i)   Estimate (do not calculate exactly) the result of this addition calculation:

3998 + 5003

Answer: ....   (1)

NUMBER C

(ii)   Estimate the result of this subtraction:

15003 − 3998

Answer: ....   (1)

13.   (i)   Estimate the result of this multiplication:

103 × 49

Answer: ....   (1)

(ii)   Estimate the result of this division:

309 ÷ 61

Answer: ....   (1)

14.   Nikita can complete about five lines of creative writing in one minute.
There are about 30 lines on each page of his exercise book.
Estimate how long it will take him to write a five-page story.

Answer: .... minutes   (3)

15. It has taken Clare about half an hour to read 15 pages of her adventure story book.

The book has a total of 306 pages.

(i) About how long will it take Clare to read the whole book?

Give your answer to the nearest hour.

Answer: .... hours   (3)

(ii) Why is it not possible to give an accurate answer in this question?

Answer: ....

....

.... (2)

16. Estimate the length of this piece of string.

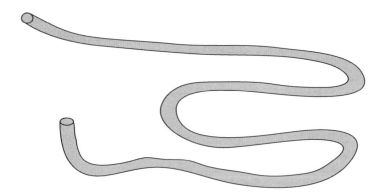

Answer: .... cm   (3)

34

D   **Fractions, decimals, percentages, ratio:** understanding fractions, decimals, percentages, and their equivalence; ratio and proportion.

1.   (i)   What fraction of this square has been shaded?

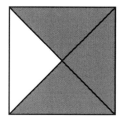

Answer: ....   (1)

(ii)   What fraction of these squares has been shaded?

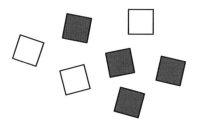

Answer: ....   (1)

2.   (i)   Shade $\frac{1}{4}$ of this shape.

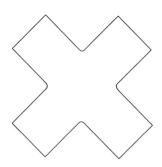

(2)

(ii)   Shade $\frac{3}{4}$ of these circles.

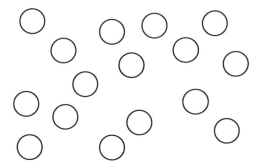

(2)

3. Shade about $\frac{1}{3}$ of this square.

(2)

4. In this strip of squares, two out of the five have been shaded.

We can write this as

$\frac{2}{5}$ ← number of squares shaded
← number of squares in the whole strip.

Sketch a similar diagram to show the fraction

$\frac{5}{8}$

(2)

5. I made a cake on Tuesday and we ate a quarter of it.

On Wednesday my brother ate half of what was left.

Find what fraction of the cake remained, using the drawing if you find it helpful.

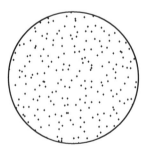

Answer: .... (3)

January 93 Q4

6. Angela has a box containing 24 chocolates.

    She gives Barbara one third of them.

    (i) How many chocolates does Barbara get?

    Answer: .... (1)

    (ii) How many chocolates are left?

    Answer: .... (1)

7. On Monday Tom had half of this pizza.

    His friend Pam had half of what was left, and Dad had half of what was left after Pam had eaten her helping.

    On the diagram draw and label each portion and work out what fraction of the whole pizza remained.

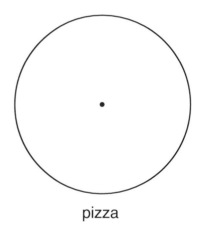

    pizza

    Answer: .... (6)

    January 91 Q13

8.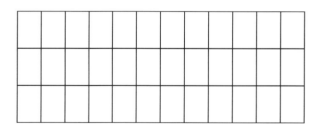

    This drawing shows a chocolate bar with 36 pieces.

    How many pieces will there be in $\frac{3}{4}$ of the bar?

    Answer: .... (2)

37

9. John is reading a book which has 240 pages.

(i) One day he read $\frac{1}{3}$ of it.
How many pages did he read?

Answer: .... (2)

(ii) The next day he read another 60 pages.
What fraction of the book is 60 pages?

Answer: .... (2)

(iii) What fraction of the book has he now read altogether?

Answer: .... (2)

(iv) How many pages has he left to read?

Answer: .... (2)

(v) If the book has 30 lines on each page, on which page will the 200th line be?

Answer: page .... (2)

November 92 Q11

10. Find $\frac{3}{4}$ of 84 cm.

Answer: .... cm   (3)   D

January 92 Q4

11. $\frac{1}{5}$ of a packet of biscuits has been eaten.

20 biscuits remain.

How many biscuits were in the full packet?

Answer: ....   (3)

January 90 Q6

12. Eletta buys 60 cm of elastic.

When it is stretched, it is $1\frac{1}{2}$ times as long.

How long is the piece of elastic when it is stretched?

Answer: .... cm   (3)

November 90 Q14

13. The price of a compact disc player was originally £500

This price has been reduced by £200

By what fraction of the original price has the compact disc player been reduced?

Answer: ....   (2)

January 91 Q8

14. The diagram shows a chessboard.

△ are white pieces.

▲ are black pieces.

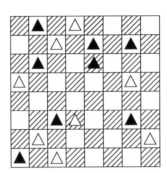

(i) What fraction of all the squares has a piece on them?

Answer: .... (2)

(ii) What fraction of all the squares does not have any piece on them?
Write the answer as a decimal.

Answer: .... (3)

(iii) If $\frac{3}{4}$ of the squares had pieces on them, how many pieces would be used?

Answer: .... (4)

(iv) Which of the following have the same value as $\frac{3}{4}$?

$\frac{75}{100}$ 0.25 $\frac{6}{8}$ 0.125 $\frac{9}{12}$

Answer: .... (4)

January 90 Q16

15. My uncle gave me £75 and asked me to save $\frac{2}{3}$ of it.

How much did I save?

Answer: £ .... (3)

November 93 Q10

16. My dog eats $\frac{2}{3}$ of a can of dog food each day.

How many cans of dog food would be required to feed 6 dogs if they were allowed $\frac{2}{3}$ of a can each?

Answer: .... (2)

November 91 Q9

17. (i) I eat $\frac{2}{5}$ of an apple.

What fraction of the apple is left?

Answer: .... (1)

(ii) Write down the smallest of these fractions.

$$\frac{1}{4} \qquad \frac{1}{3} \qquad \frac{1}{6} \qquad \frac{1}{8}$$

Answer: .... (2)

January 95 Q5

18. Which is bigger, $\frac{1}{8}$ or $\frac{1}{9}$?

Answer: .... (2)

November 90 Q9

NUMBER

D

19. Which is bigger, $\frac{3}{4}$ or $\frac{2}{3}$?

Answer: .... (2)

November 90 Q10

20. Write these fractions in order of **increasing** size.

$$\frac{1}{3} \qquad \frac{3}{4} \qquad \frac{1}{2} \qquad \frac{2}{3} \qquad \frac{1}{4}$$

.... (2)

21.

On this number line,

(i) mark $\frac{1}{2}$ with letter **A**. (1)

(ii) mark $\frac{1}{4}$ with letter **B**. (1)

(iii) mark $\frac{2}{3}$ with letter **C**. (2)

(iv) mark $1\frac{1}{4}$ with letter **D**. (2)

22. How many halves are there in $3\frac{1}{2}$?

Answer: .... (1)

23. How many quarters are there in $1\frac{1}{4}$?

Answer: .... (1)

November 90 Q1

24. Emily has drawn a machine which finds equivalent fractions.

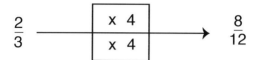

$$\frac{2}{3} \longrightarrow \boxed{\begin{array}{c} \text{x } 4 \\ \hline \text{x } 4 \end{array}} \longrightarrow \frac{8}{12}$$

(i) Fill in the details to show how the machine can change $\frac{1}{2}$ into twelfths.

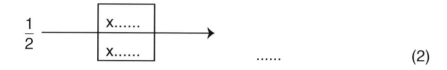

$$\frac{1}{2} \longrightarrow \boxed{\begin{array}{c} \text{x} \ldots\ldots \\ \hline \text{x} \ldots\ldots \end{array}} \longrightarrow \quad \ldots\ldots$$

(2)

(ii) Fill in the details to show how the machine can change $\frac{1}{4}$ to twelfths.

$$\frac{1}{4} \longrightarrow \boxed{\begin{array}{c} \text{x} \ldots\ldots \\ \hline \text{x} \ldots\ldots \end{array}} \longrightarrow \quad \ldots\ldots$$

(2)

25. (i) Change $\frac{3}{5}$ to tenths.

Answer: .... (2)

(ii) Change $\frac{3}{4}$ to twentieths.

Answer: .... (2)

26. Which is larger, $\frac{4}{5}$ or $\frac{17}{20}$? *(Show how you do this!)*

Answer: .... (2)

NUMBER

D

Note: Although the writing of a fraction in its simplest form may be covered in Year 7, it is included here for convenience since it features in some past questions.

27.   David has drawn a machine which simplifies fractions.

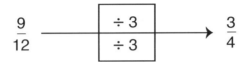

$$\frac{9}{12} \longrightarrow \boxed{\begin{array}{c} \div 3 \\ \div 3 \end{array}} \longrightarrow \frac{3}{4}$$

(i)   Fill in the details to show how the machine can change $\frac{8}{12}$ to its simplest form.

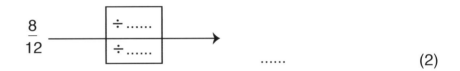

$$\frac{8}{12} \longrightarrow \boxed{\begin{array}{c} \div \ldots\ldots \\ \div \ldots\ldots \end{array}} \longrightarrow \qquad \ldots\ldots$$

(2)

(ii)   Fill in the details to show how the machine can change $\frac{18}{20}$ to its simplest form.

$$\frac{18}{20} \longrightarrow \boxed{\begin{array}{c} \div \ldots\ldots \\ \div \ldots\ldots \end{array}} \longrightarrow \qquad \ldots\ldots$$

(2)

28.   Write these fractions in their simplest forms:

(i) $\frac{12}{16}$

Answer: ....   (2)

(ii) $\frac{4}{20}$

Answer: ....   (1)

(iii) $\frac{9}{15}$

Answer: ....   (1)

29.

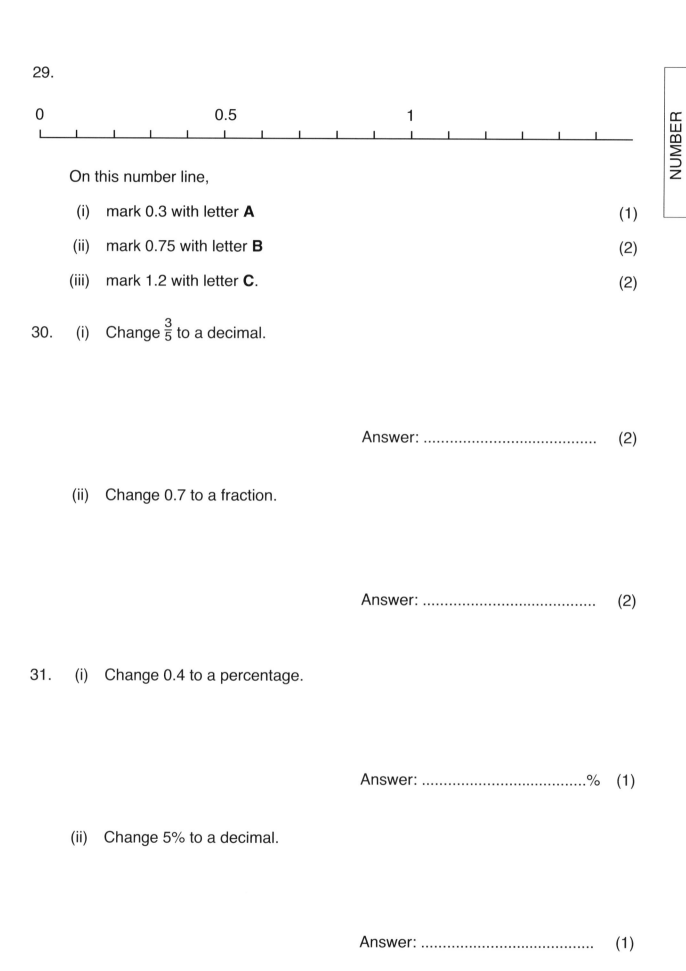

On this number line,

    (i)   mark 0.3 with letter **A**   (1)

    (ii)   mark 0.75 with letter **B**   (2)

    (iii) mark 1.2 with letter **C**.   (2)

30.   (i)   Change $\frac{3}{5}$ to a decimal.

                          Answer: ....   (2)

    (ii) Change 0.7 to a fraction.

                          Answer: ....   (2)

31.   (i)   Change 0.4 to a percentage.

                          Answer: ....%   (1)

    (ii) Change 5% to a decimal.

                          Answer: ....   (1)

32.　(i)　Change $\frac{4}{5}$ to a percentage.

Answer: .... %　(2)

(ii)　Change 13% to a fraction.

Answer: ....　(1)

33.

0   100%

On this percentage scale,

(i)　mark 50% with letter **A**　(1)

(ii)　mark 85% with letter **B**　(2)

(iii)　mark 5% with letter **C**.　(2)

34.　These are the marks which Emma scored in some tests.

Maths $\frac{65}{100}$　French 62%　English $\frac{33}{50}$　Science 64%　History $\frac{13}{20}$

(i)　What percentage did Emma score in

(a)　Maths　Answer: .... %　(1)

(b)　English　Answer: .... %　(1)

(c)　History?　Answer: .... %　(1)

(ii)　In which subject did Emma get the highest percentage?

Answer: ....　(1)

November 93 Q12

46

35. 1000 people took part in a survey carried out by a car manufacturer to help them select their colour range for the next season.

Some of the results are shown in the table.

(i) Using the clues below, complete the table.

selected colour	number of people	popularity position
black	200	....
red	....	....
white	....	2nd
blue	30	....
grey	....	4th
champagne	....	....

15% of those surveyed chose grey.

The number who chose grey was $1\frac{1}{2}$ times the number who chose champagne.

Of those remaining, 20 more chose red than those who chose white.

(8)

(ii) What percentage of those surveyed chose one of the three most popular colours?

Answer: .... % (2)

(iii) The company decides to restrict its range to just five colours.

Which colour would most likely be removed from their list?

Answer: .... (1)

Specimen 94 Q13

36. One Sunday at Clare's church, 50% of the people were women and 25% were men.

(i) What percentage of the total was children?

Answer: .... % (2)

Altogether Clare counted 120 people at church that day.

(ii) How many women were there?

Answer: .... (1)

(iii) How many men were there?

Answer: .... (1)

Another Sunday there were 150 people at church.
30 of them were children.

(iv) What percentage of the total on this Sunday was children?

Answer: .... % (2)

November 97 Q8

37.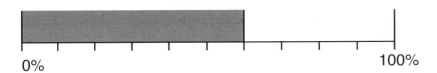

0%   100%

(i) What percentage has been shaded on this scale?

Answer: .... % (1)

(ii) What is this written as a decimal?

Answer: .... (1)

(iii) What is this written as a fraction in its simplest form?

Answer: .... (1)

38. Identical pencil cases are sold for £1 at each of four shops in a town.

During the sale, the prices of the pencil cases are reduced as shown.

PENNIBS & CO.
$\frac{1}{3}$ off all
pencil cases

J SMITH & SON
everything
reduced by
25%

BOOKS GALORE
all prices down
by $\frac{1}{4}$

BITS AND BOBS
30% off
all stock

At two of the shops the sale price of the pencil cases is the same.

Draw rings round the names of these two shops.   (3)

January 97 Q13

39. 25% of my stamp collection is French.

I have 200 stamps.

How many of my stamps are French?

Answer: ....   (2)

November 92 Q7

40. These are Ali's marks in some tests.

Give each mark as a percentage.

subject	mark	percentage
English	$\frac{83}{100}$	.... %
Maths	$\frac{25}{50}$	.... %
Science	$\frac{15}{20}$	.... %
Art	$\frac{9}{10}$	.... %

(4)

November 96 Q14

49

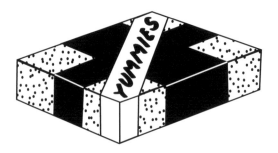

41.

(i) 25% of the sweets in a box are chocolates.

There are 36 sweets in the box.

How many are chocolates?

Answer: .... (2)

(ii) In another box there are 50 sweets, of which 10 are chocolates.

(a) What fraction of these sweets is chocolates?

Answer: .... (1)

(b) What is this as a percentage?

Answer: .... % (1)

January 95 Q7

42. Write $\frac{7}{10}$ as a percentage.

Answer: .... % (2)

November 91 Q3

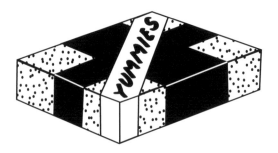

43.

A bag contains 20 balls.

50% of the balls are blue.

$\frac{1}{4}$ of the balls are red.

2 of the balls are green.

The rest of the balls are yellow.

(i) How many balls are yellow?

Answer: .... (3)

(ii) What percentage of the balls is yellow?

Answer: .... % (2)

January 98 Q13 (a)

44. The children in Ben's school are collecting money for charity.

They hope to raise £800

So far they have raised 60% of that amount.

£0   £800

   (i)   Show this by shading on the diagram. (2)

   (ii) How much have they raised so far?

Answer: £ .... (2)

January 97 Q9

45. Zara has asked all 50 girls in her year group to name their favourite pet.

These are the results.

favourite pet	number of girls
dog	24
cat	19
rabbit	7

   (i)   What percentage of the girls likes cats best?

Answer: .... % (2)

   (ii) What fraction, in its simplest form, likes dogs best?

Answer: .... (2)

46. 50 g of cornflakes contain the following:

carbohydrate	42 g
protein	4 g
fat	2 g
fibre	1 g
sodium	0.5 g
vitamins	0.5 g

(i)   What fraction of cornflakes is fibre?

Answer: ....   (1)

(ii)   What fraction of cornflakes is protein?
       Give your answer in its simplest form.

Answer: ....   (2)

(iii) What percentage of cornflakes is carbohydrate?

Answer: .... %   (2)

(iv)   What mass of carbohydrate is in 200 g of cornflakes?

Answer: .... g   (2)

November 94 Q9

53

47. The ingredients in a new chocolate bar, weighing 75 grams, are

24 g fudge

15 g raisins

18 g nuts

6 g wafer

The rest of the bar is chocolate.

(i)   What is the mass of the chocolate?

Answer: .... g   (2)

(ii) (a)   What fraction of the total mass is raisins?
Give your answer in its simplest form.

Answer: ....   (2)

(b)   Write this as a percentage.

Answer: .... %   (1)

(iii) (a)   What fraction of the total mass is nuts?
Give your answer in its simplest form.

Answer: ....   (2)

(b)   Write this as a percentage.

Answer: .... %   (1)

(iv) A shopkeeper buys the new chocolate bars for £4.56 per box in boxes
of 24

(a)   What does one bar cost the shopkeeper?

Answer: .... pence   (1)

He sells the bars for 23p each.

(b)   For how much does he sell a box of 24 bars?

Answer: £ .... (1)

(c)   What is his profit on each box?

Answer: .... pence (1)

February 94 Q14

48.   (i)   Eggs contain 10% fat and 12% protein.
      The remainder is water.
      What percentage of an egg is water?

Answer: .... % (2)

      (ii)   Every 50 g of skimmed milk contains the following:

fat	1 g
protein	18 g
carbohydrate	26 g
water	5 g

What fraction of skimmed milk is

(a)   fat

Answer: .... (1)

(b)   protein?

Answer: .... (2)

(iii)   Write the two fractions in your answers to part (ii) above as percentages.

Answer: (a) fat .... %   (b) protein .... % (4)

January 92 Q13

55

49. Angela asks each of the 200 girls in her school which is her favourite colour. These are the results:

favourite colour	number of children
red	100
blue	50
green	40
yellow	10

Mrs Jones wants to know what fraction of the girls in her school likes each colour.

Mrs Smith prefers to have the choices as percentages of the girls.

Angela has worked out the answers for red as a favourite colour.

Complete the others in the same way.

colour	fraction of girls	% of girls
red	$\frac{100}{200} = \frac{1}{2}$	50% ....
blue	....	....
green	....	....
yellow	....	....

(8)

50.

Anyprice

SALE

$\frac{1}{4}$ OFF

ALL GOODS

Maximarket

SALE

ALL GOODS

30% OFF!

NUMBER

D

In both *Anyprice* and *Maximarket*, personal stereos usually cost £60

(i)   What is the saving in *Anyprice*?

Answer: £ ....   (2)

(ii)   What is the sale price in *Maximarket*?

Answer: £ ....   (4)

November 98 Q3(b)

51.   Which of the following have the value of one quarter?

$\frac{2}{8}$ $\frac{3}{4}$ 0.25   0.75   0.4

Answer: ....   (2)

January 92 Q5

57

52. Mrs Harvey has a set of fraction dominoes.

Her maths class uses them to practise fractions, decimals and percentages.

Where dominoes are put together, the fractions, decimals or percentages have to be equivalent.

Lucy has these dominoes:

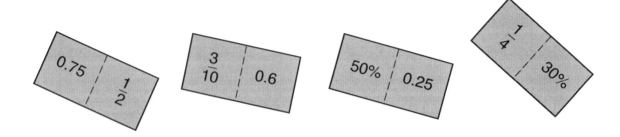

She arranges them on the table like this:

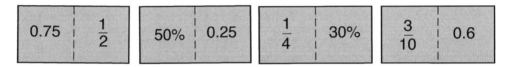

Mrs Harvey checks and says Lucy has got them all right.

(i) George has these dominoes:

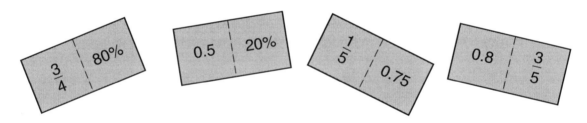

He also arranges them correctly.

Fill in the values on the dominoes to show how he arranges them.

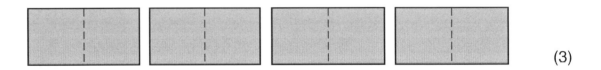

(3)

(ii)   Alice has these dominoes:

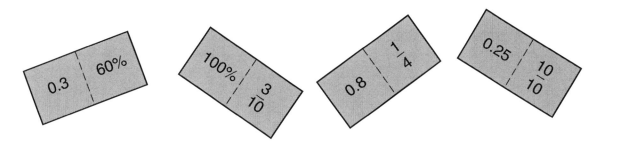

        Arrange Alice's dominoes so she gets them in the correct places.

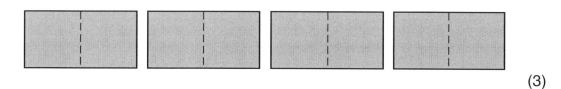

(3)

(iii)   Tom also gets his right.

        His dominoes include 25%, $\frac{3}{4}$ and 0.7

        Make up other numbers for Tom's dominoes and draw a correct arrangement.

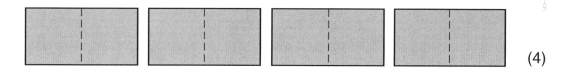

(4)

November 97 Q19

53. Complete the following:

(i) $\frac{3}{5} = \frac{}{10}$

(ii) $\frac{3}{4} = \frac{}{20}$

(iii) $\frac{3}{5} = 0.\,\text{.......}$

(iv) $\frac{3}{4} = 0.\,\text{.........}$

(v) $\frac{3}{5} = \text{.........}\ \%$

(vi) $\frac{3}{4} = \text{.........}\ \%$

(6)

January 93 Q10

54. Complete the table, showing the equivalent fractions, decimals and percentages.

fraction (in simplest form)	$\frac{1}{2}$	....	....	....	$\frac{7}{10}$
decimal	....	0.25	....	0.1	....
percentage	50%	....	75%	....	....

(9)

January 99 Q11(a)

55. (i) Mark with an **X** a point approximately $\frac{1}{3}$ of the way along the line from **P**.

P_____ (1)

(ii) Mark with an **X** a point approximately 75% of the way along the line from **Q**.

Q_____ (1)

(iii) Mark with an **X** a point approximately 0.5 of the way along the line from **R**.

R_____ (1)

November 98 Q1(b)

60

56. The drawing shows woodlice in a choice chamber.

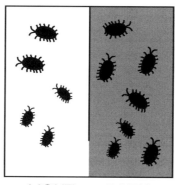

LIGHT   DARK

(i)   How many woodlice are in the light side?

Answer: ....   (1)

(ii) What fraction of the woodlice are in the dark side?

Answer: ....   (2)

(iii) What is the ratio of woodlice in the light to woodlice in the dark?

Answer: .... : ....   (2)

57. This pictogram shows the numbers of boys and girls in the class.

boys   ♀ ♀ ♀ ♀ ♀ ♀ ♀

girls   ♀ ♀ ♀ ♀ ♀ ♀ ♀ ♀ ♀ ♀ ♀

one symbol represents one child

What is the ratio of boys to girls?

Answer: .... : ....   (2)

58. This drawing shows Alison's garden:

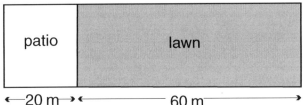

   (i)   What fraction of Alison's garden is patio?

                        Answer: ....   (1)

   (ii) What is the ratio

                  area of the patio : area of lawn?

                        Answer: .... : ....   (2)

59. William's dogs, Salt, Pepper and Mustard, find a box of 20 biscuits.
   Salt and Pepper eat 7 biscuits each and Mustard eats the rest.

   (i)   How many biscuits does Mustard eat?

                        Answer: ....   (1)

   (ii) What is the ratio of the numbers of biscuits eaten by the dogs?

            Answer: Salt .... : Pepper .... : Mustard...........   (2)

60. Anna is reading a book with 240 pages.
   So far she has read 100 pages.
   What is the ratio

                  pages Anna has read : pages still to be read?

   Simplify your answer if possible.

                        Answer: .... : ....   (2)

STRAND 2: CALCULATIONS

A **Number operations:** understanding number operations; relationships between operations

1. On this number line, an addition fact is shown: $5 + 7 = 12$

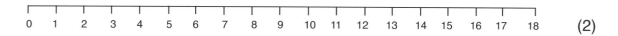

On the number line below, show the addition fact $8 + 9 = $ ....
in the same way.

```
 ┬  ┬  ┬  ┬  ┬  ┬  ┬  ┬  ┬  ┬  ┬  ┬  ┬  ┬  ┬  ┬  ┬  ┬  ┬
 0  1  2  3  4  5  6  7  8  9  10 11 12 13 14 15 16 17 18
```
(2)

2. What is the sum of 23 and 38?

Answer: .... (1)

3. Find the total of 129, 32 and 41

Answer: .... (2)

4. Amy has three lengths of string: 30 cm, 42 cm and 17 cm.

What length does she have altogether?

Answer: .... cm (2)

5. Four stones have masses of 5.3 kg, 2.9 kg, 1.4 kg and 6.8 kg.

What is their total mass?

Answer: .... kg (2)

6. Emma's height on her last birthday was 161 cm. Her height has increased by 5 cm.

What is her height now?

Answer: .... cm (1)

63

7. On this number line, a subtraction fact is shown: $15 - 6 = 9$

On the number line below, show the subtraction fact $14 - 8 =$ ....
in the same way.

(2)

8. Take 14 away from 32

Answer: .... (1)

9. Subtract 3.4 from 4.8

Answer: .... (1)

10. Ben had £12 in his pocket money savings last Saturday.

Since then the amount has decreased by £3

How much does he have now?

Answer: £ .... (1)

11. Chlöe has 84 small dolls.

Belinda has 57 dolls.

How many more dolls than Belinda does Chlöe have?

Answer: .... (1)

12. Alfonso's sunflower has grown to a height of 2.3 metres.

Lola's sunflower is not as tall and the difference between the heights of the sunflowers is 0.4 metres.

How tall is Lola's sunflower?

Answer: .... m (1)

13. Fill in the missing numbers.

   (i)   25 + 7 = ☐   (1)

   (ii) 17 + ☐ = 42   (1)

   (iii) ☐ + 9 = 20   (1)

14. Two numbers have a sum of 34
    One of the numbers is 25
    What is the other number?

                                   Answer: .... (1)

15. Give an example of two numbers which added together give 100

                                   Answer: .... and .... (1)

16. Find the missing numbers.

   (i)   8 + ☐ + 17 = 40

                                   Answer: .... (1)

   (ii) 15 + 36 + ☐ = 100

                                   Answer: .... (1)

17. Find all the totals you can make by adding together two or more of these numbers.

                 7   13   22   38

   Answer: ....

            ....

            ....

            .... (6)

18. Fill in the missing numbers.

   (i) $31 - 19 = \boxed{}$ (1)

   (ii) $56 - \boxed{} = 38$ (1)

   (iii) $\boxed{} - 17 = 20$ (1)

A

CALCULATIONS

19. The difference between two numbers is 17
    The larger number is 42
    What is the smaller number?

                              Answer: .... (1)

20. What must I take from 70 to leave 54?

                              Answer: .... (1)

21. What must be added to 3.5 to get 4.2?

                              Answer: .... (1)

22. Find the missing numbers.

   (i) $8 - 2 = 12 - \boxed{}$ (1)

   (ii) $47 - \boxed{} = 33 - 7$ (1)

23. Give an example of two numbers which have a difference of 12

                              Answer: .... (2)

24. Here is an **addition fact**:

- addition facts come in pairs
- for each pair of addition facts, there is a pair of **subtraction facts**

Using the same numbers 9, 12 and 21 in each fact, complete the other three addition / subtraction facts.

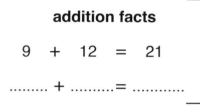
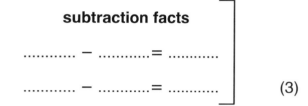

addition facts

9 + 12 = 21

.... + ...= ....

subtraction facts

.... – ....= ....

.... – ....= .... (3)

25. (i) Is 9 + 5 the same as 5 + 9?

Answer: .... (1)

(ii) Is 9 − 5 the same as 5 − 9?

Answer: .... (1)

26. A known number fact is 3 + 8 = 11

Use this fact to help you to write the answers.

(i) 30 + 80 = ... (1)

(ii) 0.3 + 0.8 = ... (1)

(iii) 11 − 8 = ... (1)

(iv) 1100 − 300 = ... (1)

(v) 1.1 − 0.8 = ... (1)

27. (i) What must I add to 8.4 to get 9.2?

Answer: .... (1)

(ii) What must I subtract from 340 to get 290?

Answer: .... (1)

A

CALCULATIONS

28. What is the missing number $\boxed{}$?

$$23 + 9 = \boxed{} - 6$$

Answer: .... (2)

February 94 Q2

A

CALCULATIONS

29. Find the missing numbers.

(i) $18 + 29 = 64 - \boxed{}$

(ii) $28 - 17 = 50 - \boxed{}$

(iii) $47 + 18 = \boxed{} - 20$

(iv) $103 - \boxed{} = 32 + 19$ (4)

30. (i) What is 24 more than 27?

Answer: .... (1)

(ii) What is 54 less than 100?

Answer: .... (1)

31. (i) What is the sum of 19 and 26?

Answer: .... (1)

(ii) What is the difference between 19 and 26?

Answer: .... (1)

(iii) How many more than 19 is 26?

Answer: .... (1)

32. Complete these multiplication strips.

X	1	2	3	4	5	6	7	8	9
5			15						
8							56		

(4)

33. (i) What is 7 times 11?

Answer: .... (1)

(ii) What is the product of 9 and 7?

Answer: .... (1)

34. (i) Write two multiples of 4 between 21 and 30

Answer: .... (2)

(ii) Is 56 a multiple of

(a) 8   Answer: .... (1)

(b) 9   Answer: .... (1)

(c) 7?   Answer: .... (1)

35. 37 × 102 = 37 × 100 + 37 × 2

= 3700 + 74

= 3774

Do this calculation in the same way.

23 × 101 = ...

....

.... (3)

69

36. (i)   Write the products of these numbers.

     4 × 9 = ...   7 × 8 = ...   (2)

     (ii) Write the missing numbers in these multiplication facts.

     .... × 9 = 72   6 × .... = 54   (2)

37. Find these products.

     (i)   45 × 10   Answer: .... (1)

     (ii) 37 × 0   Answer: .... (1)

     (iii) 83 × 1   Answer: .... (1)

38. (i)   Is this statement true?

           31 × 4 = 31 + 31 + 31 + 31

                                    Answer: .... (1)

     (ii) What is the value of 31 × 4?

                                    Answer: .... (1)

39. The number 12 can be represented as an array of dots.

           O O O O
           O O O O   3 rows of 4 dots (3 × 4)
           O O O O

     Represent the number 12 in a different way.

                                                                        (2)

40. This number line shows the multiplication fact

$$4 \times 3 = 12$$

(i) On the number line below, show the multiplication fact

$$3 \times 4 = 12$$

(2)

(ii) On the number line below, show the multiplication fact

$$4 \times 7 = 28$$

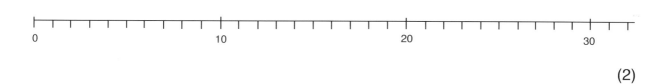

(2)

41. The machine below multiplies by three

INPUT   4   ────>── ×3 ──>────   12   OUTPUT

         7   ──────────>──────   ....

         ....   ──────────>──────   27

         24   ──────────>──────   ....

Fill in the missing input and output numbers.   (3)

42. Which single machine would do the same job as these two?

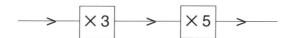

Answer: ──────>── [.......] ──>──   (2)

43. (i) Complete this multiplication square.

X	1	2	3	4	5	6	7	8	9
1	1	2	3	4	5	6	7	8	9
2	2	4	6	8	10	12	14	16	18
3	3	6	9	12	15	18	21	24	27
4	4	8	12	16	20	24	28	32	36
5	5	10	15	20	25	30	.....	40	45
6	6	12	18	24	30	.....	.....	48	54
7	7	14	21	28	35	.....	49	.....	.....
8	8	16	24	32	40	.....	56	.....	.....
9	9	18	27	36	45	54	.....	72	81

(5)

(ii) Study the shaded square representing the multiplication fact

$$4 \times 8 = 32$$

We can use this same information to show that 32 divides exactly by 4 and by 8

Use the multiplication square to answer the following questions:

(a) Does 56 divide exactly by 8?

Answer: .... (1)

(b) Does 45 divide exactly by 7?

Answer: .... (1)

(c) Does 23 divide exactly by *any* of the numbers 2 to 9?

Answer: .... (1)

(d) What is the remainder when 25 is divided by 6?

(Hint: look along the 6 times strip and see which multiple of 6 is the nearest below 25 and subtract that from 25)

Answer: .... (1)

(e) What is the remainder when 30 is divided by 4?

Answer: .... (1)

44. (i) What is 63 divided by 7?

Answer: .... (1)

(ii) How many times will 8 go into 72?

Answer: .... (1)

45. (i) Share 18 sweets between 6 children.
How many will each child receive?

Answer: .... (1)

(ii) How many groups of 7 children can be made with a school of 63 children?

Answer: .... (1)

46. (i) Is 342 divisible by 3?

Answer: .... (1)

(ii) How did you know?

Answer: ....

.... (2)

47. (i)   Is 23145 divisible by 5?   Answer: .... (1)

     (ii) Is 23145 divisible by 3?   Answer: .... (1)

     (iii) Is 23145 divisible by 9?   Answer: .... (1)

48. The fraction $\frac{3}{4}$ can be thought of as '3 out of 4' or '3 divided by 4', or 'three lots of a quarter'.

     Write the fractions which are equivalent to

     (i)   3 divided by 5   Answer: .... (1)

     (ii)   4 divided by 7   Answer: .... (1)

     (iii) 7 divided by 4   Answer: .... (1)

49. $\frac{1}{3}$ of 24 is equivalent to 24 ÷ 3 and $\frac{24}{3}$

     Write similar equivalent forms of $\frac{1}{5}$ of 40

     Answer: .... and .... (2)

50. Multiplying by $\frac{1}{3}$ is the same as dividing by 3

     Multiplying by 3 is the same as dividing by $\frac{1}{3}$

     Make use of this information to calculate the following:

     (i) $\frac{1}{3} \times 30$

                                   Answer: .... (1)

     (ii) $30 \div \frac{1}{3}$

                                   Answer: .... (1)

74

51. Here is a **multiplication fact**:
- multiplication facts come in pairs
- for each pair of multiplication facts, there is a pair of **division facts**

Using the same numbers 6, 9 and 54 in each fact, complete the other three multiplication / division facts.

multiplication facts	**division facts**
6 × 9 = 54	.... ÷ .... = ...
.... × .... = ...	.... ÷ .... = ... (3)

52. (i)   Is 9 × 3 the same as 3 × 9?

Answer: .... (1)

(ii)   Is 9 ÷ 3 the same as 3 ÷ 9?

Answer: .... (1)

53. A known division fact is 24 ÷ 8 = 3

Use this fact to help you to write the following answers:

(i)   240 ÷ 8 = ... (1)

(ii)   24 ÷ 80 = ... (2)

(iii)   2400 ÷ 80 = ... (1)

(iv)   24 ÷ 0.8 = ... (2)

(v)   2.4 ÷ 8 = ... (2)

54. Find the answers to these divisions.

(i)   450 ÷ 10   Answer: .... (1)

(ii)   45 ÷ 10   Answer: .... (1)

(iii)   45 ÷ 100   Answer: .... (2)

(iv)   4.5 ÷ 100   Answer: .... (2)

A

CALCULATIONS

55. (i) This number line shows the division fact 15 ÷ 3 = 5

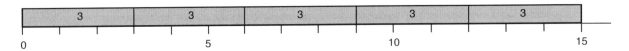

3 goes into 15 five times, exactly.

On this number line, show the division fact 12 ÷ 4 = 3

(2)

(ii) This number line shows what happens when we divide 20 by 6

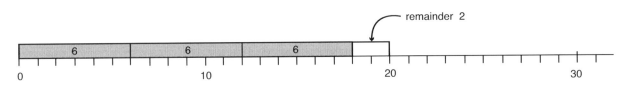

20 ÷ 6 → 3 remainder 2

On this number line, show what happens when we divide 24 by 7

(2)

56. A minibus can carry 14 children.

50 children are being taken to a concert.

(i) How many minibuses will be needed?

Answer: .... (2)

(ii) How many spare seats will there be?

Answer: .... (2)

CALCULATIONS

A

57. Miss Pringle has 100 sweets and is making up bags of 8 sweets.

   (i)   How many bags will she be able to make up?

                                        Answer: ....   (3)

   (ii) How many extra sweets will she have?

                                        Answer: ....   (2)

A

CALCULATIONS

58. Ann, Bella and Carrie have been asked to share £17 between five children.
    They give these answers:

         Ann: £3.4   Bella: £3$\frac{2}{5}$ Carrie: £3 remainder £2

   (i)   Which answer do you think is most appropriate in this case?

                                        Answer: £ ....   (1)

   (ii) Explain why.

         Answer: ....

         ....   (2)

59. Dora, Erica and Fatima have been asked to find how many pizzas will be
    needed when 25 children eat a quarter of a pizza each.
    They give these answers:

         Dora: 6.25   Erica: 6$\frac{1}{4}$ Fatima: 6 remainder 1

   (i)   Which answer do you think is most appropriate in this case?

                                        Answer: ....   (1)

   (ii) Explain why.

         Answer: ....

         ....   (2)

77

60. Georgina, Harriet and Iona have been asked to find how long each piece of wood will be if a 140 cm length is cut into 8 equal pieces.

They give their answers as

Georgina: 17.5   Harriet: $17\frac{1}{2}$ Iona: 17 remainder 4

(i)   Which answer do you think is the most appropriate in this case?

Answer: .... (2)

(ii)   Explain why.

Answer: ....

.... (2)

61. In multiplication we can replace a [× 6] machine by

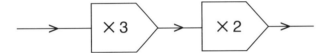

In the same way, we can replace a [÷ 6] machine by

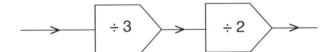

This can be a very useful idea when dividing by larger numbers.

(i)   Suggest two machines which might replace [÷ 21]

Answer: (2)

(ii)   Suggest two machines which might replace [÷ 54]

Answer: (2)

62. Fill in the missing numbers.

   (i)   24 ÷ 3 = ... (1)

   (ii) 36 ÷ .... = 9 (1)

   (iii) .... ÷ 5 = 20 (2)

   (iv) 30 ÷ 6 = ... ÷ 8 (2)

63. We can multiply a number by 32, by doubling five times.
    Fill in the gaps here.

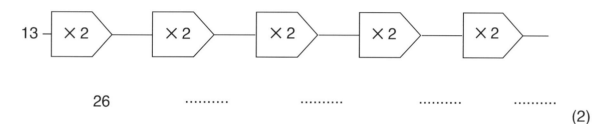

        26   ....
                                                                              (2)

64. Keep halving, starting with 480, until you reach an odd number.

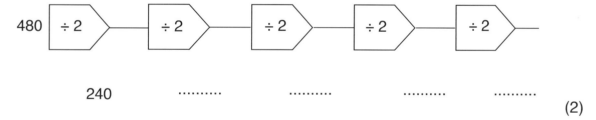

        240   ....
                                                                              (2)

65. (i) Keep on doubling, starting with 2, until you get a number greater than
         100

         Answer: 2 → .... (2)

    (ii) Keep on halving, starting with 420, until you reach an odd number.

         Answer: 420 → .... (2)

79

66. This example shows one way of multiplying 123 by 32

×	123			result
	100	20	3	
32 **30**	3000	600	90	3690
2	200	40	6	246
				3936

In the same way, multiply 241 by 29

×	241			result
	200	40	1	
29 **20**				
9				

(4)

67. Complete the missing numbers for this pair of inverse machines.

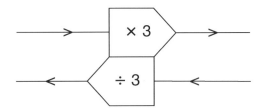

5   ....

....   21

18   ....   (3)

B **Mental strategies:** developing mental calculation strategies, including deriving new facts from known facts

Note
For all questions in this section you should do no written working, but simply write the answers. Do all the calculations in your head. Check that each answer is sensible.

1. Fill in the missing numbers.

    (i)   31 + 99 = ... (1)

    (ii) 132 + 17 = ... (1)

    (iii) 398 + 103 = ... (1)

    (iv) 28 + 42 + 77 = ... (1)

    (v)   55 + ... = 100 (1)

2. Fill in the missing numbers.

    (i)   80 − 39 = ... (1)

    (ii) 54 − 29 = ... (1)

    (iii) 90 − 41 = ... (1)

    (iv) 152 − 99 = ... (1)

    (v)   67 − .... = 33 (1)

3. (i)   Which number should I add to 45 to get 92? .... (1)

    (ii) What must I subtract from 80 to get 37? .... (1)

    (iii) What is the sum of 34, 27 and 59? .... (1)

    (iv) What is the difference between 63 and 29? .... (1)

    (v)   What do I get when I take 74 from 180? .... (1)

4.   Fill in the missing numbers.

   (i) $2 \times 19 = $ ....   (1)

   (ii) $5 \times 31 = $ ....   (1)

   (iii) $29 \times 6 = $ ....   (1)

   (iv) $11 \times 13 = $ ....   (1)

   (v) $4 \times $ .... $ = 84$ (1)

5.   Fill in the missing numbers.

   (i) $36 \div 3 = $ ....   (1)

   (ii) $100 \div 4 = $ ....   (1)

   (iii) $420 \div 6 = $ ....   (1)

   (iv) $360 \div 4 = $ ....   (1)

   (v) $180 \div $ .... $ = 30$ (1)

6.   (i)   Which number should I multiply by 4 to get 60? ....   (1)

   (ii)   What must I divide 54 by to get 18? ....   (1)

   (iii)   What is the product of 3, 4 and 5? ....   (1)

   (iv)   How many times does 5 go into 200? ....   (1)

   (v)   What do I get when I divide 54 by 3? ....   (1)

7.   Fill in the missing numbers.

   (i) $4.1 + 3.9 = $ ....   (1)

   (ii) $8.0 - 4 \cdot 2 = $ ....   (1)

   (iii) $3 \times 0.99 = $ ....   (1)

   (iv) $6 \div 4 = $ ....   (1)

   (v) $1.2 \div $ .... $ = 0.4$ (1)

8. (i) What is the cost of nine biscuits which cost three pence each?

Answer: .... pence (1)

(ii) Eight sweets cost 96 pence altogether. What is the cost of one sweet?

Answer: .... pence (1)

(iii) Rory started with 63 marbles.
He has lost 18 marbles
How many does he have left?

Answer: .... (1)

9. There are 342 children in a school.
One day 69 children are absent.
How many are at school that day?

Answer: .... (2)

January 96 Q1

10. A car is 3.4m long and a caravan is 4.9m long.
What is the total length?

Answer: .... m (2)

11. Ann cuts a 2.1m length from a 4m piece of ribbon.
What length is left?

Answer: .... m (2)

12. There are 46 people on a bus.
At the next stop 18 of them get off and 13 people get on.
How many are now on the bus?

Answer: .... (3)

November 96 Q2

13. What is the cost of 11 chocolate bars, costing 23 pence each?

Answer: .... pence (2)

CALCULATIONS B

83

14. How many books costing £3.99 each can be bought for £20?

Answer: .... (2)

15. (i) What is the cost of 15 sweets which cost four pence each?

Answer: .... pence (1)

(ii) Five biscuits cost 90 pence altogether.
What is the cost of one biscuit?

Answer: .... pence (1)

(iii) Amanda started with 50 beetles.
She has lost 11 beetles.
How many does she have left?

Answer: .... (1)

16. Complete these statements.

(i) 20 × 400 = ... (1)

(ii) 21 × 400 = ... (1)

(iii) 20 × 399 = ... (2)

(iv) 19 × 400 = ... (2)

17. (i) What is one half of 86?

Answer: .... (1)

(ii) What is one quarter of 64?

Answer: .... (1)

(iii) What is one eighth of 96?

Answer: .... (2)

18. (i) What is 90 ÷ 6?

Answer: .... (2)

(ii) What is 13 × 8?

Answer: .... (2)

19. 1.3 × 1.4 = 1.82

What is 1.82 ÷ 1.4?

Answer: .... (1)

20. What is 8.5 × 4?

Answer: .... (2)

21. 14 × 5 = 70

What is one fifth of 70?

Answer: .... (2)

22. John left home at 13:55 and reached the shops at 15:20

How long did his journey take?

Answer: .... minutes (2)

23. Willie left home at 09:45 and cycled for 55 minutes to reach his aunt's house.

At what time did he arrive?

Answer: .... (1)

24. Agatha cannot remember what time she started to watch the film *The Old Ones* but she knows that the film lasts for 1 hour and 50 minutes and that it ended at 19:05

At what time did it start?

Answer: .... (2)

25. What is the smallest number, greater than 100, which divides exactly by 3?

Answer: .... (2)

26. What is one fifth of 360?

Answer: .... (1)

85

27. $8 \times 31 = 248$

What is 16×31?

Answer: .... (2)

January 91 Q6

28. What is the missing number?

Since $16 \times 73 = 1168$

then $1.6 \times 7.3 = $ .... (2)

Specimen 94 Q2

29. Use the fact below to complete the following:

$$126 \times 49 = 6174$$

(You should not need to do any working on the paper.)

   (i) $12.6 \times 49 = $ .... (1)

   (ii) $1.26 \times 4.9 = $ .... (1)

   (iii) $6174 \div 49 = $ .... (1)

   (iv) $6174 \div 12.6 = $ .... (1)

November 95 Q16

30. Use the multiplication fact below to fill in the following blanks:

$$38 \times 30 = 1140$$

(You should not need to do any working on paper.)

   (i) $380 \times 30 \ = $ .... (1)

   (ii) $3.8 \times 30 = $ .... (1)

   (iii) $38 \times 15 = $ .... (1)

   (iv) $1140 \div 38 = $ .... (1)

   (v) $1140 \div 15 = $ .... (1)

January 96 Q9

31. 10% of £38 is £3.80

    (i)   What is 5% of £38?

                                        Answer: £ ....   (2)

    (ii) What is 2.5% of £38?

                                        Answer: £ ....   (2)

    (iii) What is 15% of £38?

                                        Answer: £ ....   (2)

32. Jimmy's pen is not working properly.

    Blots of ink have fallen onto his work, covering part of these number sentences.

    Which numbers have been covered up?

    (i) $15 \times 16 = 30 \times 8$

          $30 \times 8 = $ (..............) $\times 4$

          $30 \times 8 = 120 \times$ (..............)   (2)

    (ii) $45 \times 6 = $ (..............) $\times 3$

          $45 \times 6 = 270 \times$ (..............)   (2)

    January 98 Q7

33. (i)   Write the products of these numbers.

          (a) $8 \times 7 = $ ....   (b) $6 \times 9 = $ ....   (2)

    (ii) Write the missing numbers in these multiplication facts.

          (a) .... $\times 7 = 49$ (b) $8 \times$ .... $= 40$ (2)

87

34. Complete these multiplication facts.

    (i)   5 × 6 = ...   (ii)   4 × 9 = ...   (2)

    (iii) 3 × 7 = ...   (iv)   6 × 7 = ...   (2)

35. What is the product of 9 and 6?

                              Answer: .... (2)

January 90 Q9

36. (i)   Write the products of these numbers.

         (a)   7 × 9 = ...   (b)   6 × 8 = ...   (2)

     (ii) Write the missing numbers in these multiplication facts.

         (a)   .... × 9 = 54   (b)   7 × .... = 49   (2)

37. Fill in the missing numbers.

     (i)   35 × 6 = 70 × ....   (2)

     (ii) 100 ÷ 4 = ...÷ 8   (2)

Specimen 94 Q4

More questions involving mental strategies are to be found throughout the other sections.

88

C **Written methods:** using written calculation (pencil and paper) methods

When answering these questions, you are expected to show clearly all your working, even if you could do these in your head.

1. Add

    (i)

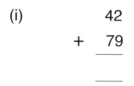

                                         Answer: .... (1)

    (ii) 78 + 53

                                           Answer: .... (2)

2. Add

    (i)
$$\begin{array}{r} 28.4 \\ +\ 13.9 \\ \hline \\ \hline \end{array}$$

                                           Answer: .... (1)

    (ii) 27.3 + 19.4

                                           Answer: .... (2)

3. Add together   3.1   1.9   and   4.7

                                           Answer: .... (2)

CALCULATIONS **C**

4. Set these out very carefully, using the column headings.

(i) 18.45 + 30.95

T   U   •   t   h

Answer: .... (2)

(ii) 10.95 + 8.7

T   U   •   t   h

Answer: .... (2)

5. Calculate

$$1.4 + 14 + 0.14$$

Answer: .... (2)

November 95 Q5

6. Add

$$91.4 + 9.14$$

Answer: .... (2)

7. Subtract

   (i)   139

        −   45

                Answer: .... (1)

   (ii) 214 − 57

                Answer: .... (2)

8. Subtract

   (i)   3.07

        −   2.95

                Answer: .... (2)

   (ii) 8.1 − 3.8

                Answer: .... (2)

9. Subtract 13.8 from 21.7

                Answer: .... (2)

CALCULATIONS
C

10. Set these out very carefully.

(i)   10.28 − 4.5

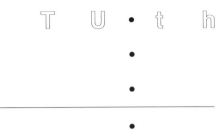

Answer: .... (2)

(ii)   24.2 − 8.75

Answer: .... (3)

11.   Which number is 5.4 less than 12.5?

Answer: .... (1)

12.   What must I add to 11.4 to get 15.0?

Answer: .... (2)

In these multiplication questions, if you usually set out your calculation in a different way, use your own method but be sure to show clearly what you are doing.

13. Multiply

    (i)
$$\begin{array}{r} 51 \\ \times \quad 8 \\ \hline \\ \hline \end{array}$$

Answer: .... (2)

    (ii) 19 × 7

Answer: .... (2)

CALCULATIONS C

14. Multiply

    (i)
$$\begin{array}{r} 2.9 \\ \times \quad 7 \\ \hline \\ \hline \end{array}$$

Answer: .... (2)

    (ii) 13.6 × 5

Answer: .... (2)

15. Multiply

$$\begin{array}{r} 123 \\ \times \quad 11 \\ \hline \end{array}$$

....

Answer: .... (3)

16. Multiply

    (i)   12.5

         ×   3

                                 Answer: .... (2)

    (ii)   1.45 × 5

                                 Answer: .... (2)

17. Multiply

    (i)   3.52

         ×   12

        ....

                                 Answer: .... (3)

    (ii)   18.7 × 2.1

                                 Answer: .... (3)

In these division questions, if you usually set out your calculation in a different way, use your own method but be sure to show clearly what you are doing.

18. Divide

    (i)   3 | 4   2

       ....

                                    Answer: .... (1)

    (ii) 6 | 2   4   6

       ....

                                    Answer: .... (1)

19. Do these divisions, setting your work out as in the example, giving your answers as decimals.

    Example: 5 | **26.0**
                             5.2

    (i)   3 | 9.6

                                    Answer: .... (2)

    (ii)   25 ÷ 4

                                    Answer: .... (2)

    (iii)   12.3 ÷ 6

                                    Answer: .... (3)

CALCULATIONS

C

20. Divide, showing clearly what you are doing, and giving your answer with a remainder as in the example.

Example:

$$4\,|\,3\ ^{3}0\ ^{2}$$
$$\underline{\quad7\ \ R\ \ 2\quad}$$

(i) $5\,|\,8\ \ 7$

Answer: .... R .... (2)

(ii) $7\,|\,2\ \ 8\ \ 3$

Answer: .... R .... (2)

21. Calculate $1.44 \div 8$

Answer: .... (2)

November 91 Q2

22. (i) Divide 8 by 4

Answer: .... (1)

(ii) Divide 4 by 8

Answer: .... (2)

96

23. Calculate

    (i)   426 × 4

Answer: .... (2)

    (ii)   1045 ÷ 5

Answer: .... (1)

November 95 Q4

24. Calculate

    (i)   3.8 × 5

Answer: .... (2)

    (ii)   3.8 ÷ 5

Answer: .... (2)

97

25. (i) What is the total cost of four books costing £3.45 each?

Answer: £ .... (2)

CALCULATIONS

C

(ii) £5.00 is shared equally between four children.
How much will each receive?

Answer: £ .... (2)

26. (i) Five identical boxes have a total mass of 4.2 kg.
What is the mass of one box?

Answer: .... kg (2)

(ii) Each box has a height of 37 centimetres.
They are placed one on top of the other.
How high is the pile?

Answer: .... cm (2)

D   Calculator methods: using a calculator

(These questions do not require the use of a calculator.)

1. Alice was asked to share £45 between six people.
    This was her calculator display:

    > 7.5

    How much money did each person receive?

    Answer: £ .... (1)

2. Beatrice's calculator shows this result:

    > 20.

    Which number has she multiplied by 8?

    Answer: .... (2)

3. Colin has divided 1 by 9
    What can you say about the decimal shown in his calculator display?

    > 0.111111111

    Answer: ....

    .... (2)

4. Dora has found the cube of 99

    > 970299.

    (i) Write this result to the nearest 1000.

    Answer: .... (1)

    (ii) Write the result to the nearest 100.

    Answer: .... (2)

99

5. Emma's calculator displayed

$$189.23574$$

(i) Write this number correct to the nearest 100.

Answer: .... (1)

(ii) Write this number correct to the nearest whole number.

Answer: .... (1)

(iii) Write this number to the nearest 10.

Answer: .... (1)

November 94 Q2

CALCULATIONS

D

6. Florence has been finding the decimal equivalents of some fractions.

$\frac{5}{17}$ 0.294117647

$\frac{14}{47}$ 0.29787234

$\frac{8}{27}$ 0.296296296

$\frac{11}{37}$ 0.297297297

(i) Place the above fractions in order of **increasing** size.

Answer: .... , ... , ... , ... (2)

(ii) What can you say about the decimal equivalents of

$\frac{8}{27}$ and $\frac{11}{37}$?

Answer: ....

.... (2)

100

7. Graham has used his calculator to find the total cost of 11 chocolate bars priced at 32 pence each.

The calculator shows

$$352.$$

What is the total cost of the chocolate bars?

Answer: £ .... (1)

8. The $\boxed{\times}$ button on Harriet's calculator is not working.

How could she use the calculator to find the answer to 600×0.5?

Answer: ....

.... (2)

9. Isla's calculator shows the display

$$-3.$$

Which number did she subtract from 5?

Answer: .... (2)

10. Jane has used her calculator to find the perimeter of a square of side 8.9 cm.
This is the display:

$$35.6$$

Suggest two reasons why Jane believes that this is a correct result.

Answer: ....

....

....

.... (3)

11. Kenny has tried to do the calculation 8.9 + 1.7

His calculator shows this result:

$$7.2$$

He realises that this cannot be correct.
Suggest what he might have done wrong.

Answer: ....

.... (2)

12. Lara did the calculation 2 ÷ 7 = and then multiplied the result by 7

She expected to get the answer 2!
The calculator display surprised her.

$$1.999999995$$

Suggest an explanation.

Answer: ....

....

.... (3)

13. Morag used her calculator whilst doing some shopping to keep a record of the money she would have left.

First she entered 20, since she started with a £20 note.

She then subtracted the cost of each item as she put it into her shopping basket.

Just before reaching the checkout she pressed = and was surprised to see this display.

$$-0.19$$

Assuming that she had pressed all the keys correctly, what does this mean?

Answer: ....

.... (2)

E   **Checking results:** checking that results of calculations are reasonable

1.   Hannah has completed the series of calculations shown in this flow chart.

Show how she can check this by doing the reverse operations.

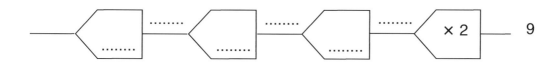

(3)

2.   Iona has multiplied 12 by $\frac{2}{3}$ and has incorrectly written the result as 9

Do the equivalent calculation of dividing by 3 and then multiplying by 2 to find the correct result.

Answer: .... (2)

3.   Complete these facts using the words **odd** or **even**:

(i)   An odd number plus an odd number always gives an

.... number.   (1)

(ii)   An even number minus an odd number always gives an

.... number.   (1)

(iii)   An odd number multiplied by an even number always gives an

.... number.   (1)

(iv)   An .... number squared is always an odd number.   (1)

103

4. Complete these statements. *(The first one is done for you as an example.)*

Example: A number ending in 5, plus a number ending in ....8......., always gives a number ending in 3

(i) A number ending in 6, plus a number ending in 3, always gives a

   number ending in .... (1)

(ii) A number ending in 7, plus a number ending in ...., always gives

   a number ending in 1 (1)

(iii) A number ending in 5, minus a number ending in 3, always gives a

   number ending in .... (1)

(iv) A number ending in 4, minus a number ending in 8, always gives a

   number ending in .... (2)

(v) A number ending in ...., minus a number ending in 7, always

   gives a number ending in 5 (2)

(vi) A number ending in 3, minus a number ending in ...., always

   gives a number ending in 4 (2)

(vii) A number ending in 4, times a number ending in 8, always gives a

   number ending in .... (1)

(viii) A number ending in 3, times a number ending in ...., always

   gives a number ending in 1 (2)

(ix) A number ending in ...., times a number ending in 7, always

   gives a number ending in 3 (2)

(x) A number ending in .... squared always gives a number ending

   in 5 (1)

On this page, you are not expected to do any written calculations!

5. Which of the numbers

    2   3   4   5   6   8   9

    will divide exactly into

    (i)   20   Answer: .... (2)

    (ii) 35   Answer: .... (2)

    (iii) 126   Answer: .... (2)

    (iv) 1000   Answer: .... (2)

    (v)   78?   Answer: .... (2)

CALCULATIONS E

6. (i)   Is 200001 divisible by

          (a)   3   Answer: (yes/no) .... (1)

          (b)   5   Answer: (yes/no) .... (1)

          (c)   9?   Answer: (yes/no) .... (1)

    (ii) Is 3014595 divisible by

          (a)   3   Answer: (yes/no) .... (1)

          (b)   5   Answer: (yes/no) .... (1)

          (c)   9?   Answer: (yes/no) .... (1)

7. (i)   What is the smallest number over 1000 which is divisible by 3?

                                    Answer: .... (1)

    (ii) What is the largest number below 1000 which is divisible by 6?

                                    Answer: .... (2)

8. Is 20400 a multiple of

    (i)   3   Answer: (yes/no) ....   (1)

    (ii) 5   Answer: (yes/no) ....   (1)

    (iii) 15   Answer: (yes/no) ....   (1)

    (iv) 8?   Answer: (yes/no) ....   (1)

9. Write four different numbers between 200 and 300 which are multiples of 3

    Answer: ....   (3)

10. Write a number between 1000 and 2000 which is a multiple of 6

                                    Answer: ....   (2)

11. Write a number between 300 and 400 which is divisible by 9

                                    Answer: ....   (2)

12. Billy has tried to multiply 1789 by 6107 and he has written the result as 10925421
    How can you tell at a glance that this is an incorrect result?

    Answer: ....

    ....   (2)

STRAND 3: SOLVING PROBLEMS

A **Decision making, strategies:** deciding which operation, which method (mental, mental with jottings, pencil and paper, calculator), which equipment

1. Decide which method you might **best** use to solve each problem:
   - mental – entirely in your head   (M)
   - mental with jottings – perhaps making a note of an intermediate result   (MJ)
   - pencil and paper – setting out a calculation, such as a long multiplication, on paper, or doing a drawing   (PP)
   - calculator – *only if all other methods are unsuitable*!   (C)

   Write M, MJ, PP or C. You do **not** need to solve the problems!

   (i)   What is the cost of ten stamps costing 29 pence each?

   Answer: .... (1)

   (ii) This pentagon has five diagonals.

   How many diagonals has a hexagon?

   Answer: .... (1)

   (iii) Find out how many videos costing £9.99 can be bought for £150

   Answer: .... (1)

   (iv) What is the product of 37 and 23?

   Answer: .... (1)

(v) Which number multiplied by itself is 361?

Answer: .... (1)

(vi) Mary bought eight chocolate bars costing 29 pence each.
How much change would she get from a £5 note?

Answer: .... (1)

(vii) What is the area of your hand?

Answer: .... (1)

(viii) Three kittens have masses 1200 g, 1123 g and 1314 g.
What is their total mass?

Answer: .... (1)

A

PROBLEMS

2. Decide which operations (+, −, ×, ÷) you would use to help you to solve these problems.

(If more than one operation would be used, write the operations in the correct order.)

Do not calculate the answer!

(i) Emily bought cards costing 59p, 79p, £1.05 and £1.35
How much change would she get from a £10 note?

Answer: £ .... (1)

(ii) Lola shared her bag of 43 sweets as fairly as possible between five friends.
How many sweets were left over?

Answer: .... (1)

(iii) William bought five chocolate bars costing 34 pence each and two packets of crisps costing 18 pence each.
How much change would he get from £5?

Answer: £ .... (1)

3. Which equipment would you use, and how would you use it, to solve these practical problems?

(i) the height of your teacher

Answer: equipment: .... (1)

method: ....

.... (1)

(ii) the distance round your waist

Answer: equipment: .... (1)

method: ....

.... (1)

(iii) the temperature of water in your bath

Answer: equipment: .... (1)

method: ....

.... (1)

(iv) the capacity of a large bucket

Answer: equipment: .... (1)

method: ....

.... (1)

(v) the length of time it would take you to run 100 m

Answer: equipment: .... (1)

method: ....

.... (1)

4. Explain clearly how you would solve these practical problems and say what equipment you would use.

(i) the mass of a cornflake

Answer: ....

....

....

....

.... (4)

(ii) the area of your hand

Answer: ....

....

....

....

.... (3)

(iii) the number of times out of a hundred that you might expect to score 6 with a biased spinner

Answer: ....

....

....

....

.... (4)

5. The signpost shows that it is 96 miles east to Stockton and 43 miles west to Homebury.

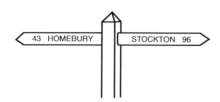

How do you work out how many miles it is from Homebury to Stockton?

Choose the correct calculation but do not work out the answer.

43×96 $96 \div 43$ $43 \div 96$

43×2 $96 - 43$ $43 + 96$

Answer: .... (1)

January 90 Q11

6. Tom has 348 stamps in his album.

John has 96 more than Tom.

How many stamps does John have?

Answer: .... (1)

January 99 Q1

7. Katie has 24 badges and Ruth has eight fewer than Katie.

They give Robin six and then share the rest equally between Alexander and Keeba.

How many will Keeba get?

Which of these calculations will be helpful? Circle them!

$24 + 8$ $24 - 8$ $24 \div 8$ 24×8

$32 - 6$ $24 + 16$ $40 - 6$ $24 - 14$

$26 \div 2$ $30 \div 2$ $34 \div 2$ $10 \div 2$

10×2 16×2 $28 \div 2$ $38 \div 2$

Answer: Keeba will get .... badges.   (4)

PROBLEMS A

111

For the questions on this page, show clearly the method you have chosen.

8. Andrew was born in 1983. How old will he be on his birthday in the year 2010?

Answer: .... (1)

November 93 Q4

9. 98 adults and 143 children go to a circus.

How many people go altogether?

Answer: .... (2)

January 97 Q1

10. Peter has been asked to put out the chairs for a concert.

There are to be 10 rows of 12 chairs.

Peter can carry 3 chairs at a time.

How many trips to the chair store will he need to do?

Answer: .... (3)

11. Which sign could you put in the box to make this calculation correct?

$$0.36 \boxed{} 100 = 36$$

Answer: .... (2)

January 91 Q9

12. Anne and Bill both collect autographs of famous authors.

Anne has 17 and Bill has 31

Two of Anne's favourite autographs are shown below.

Jack Higgins   Terry Pratchett

(i) (a) How many autographs do they have altogether?

Answer: .... (1)

(b) How many more autographs than Anne does Bill have?

Answer: .... (1)

(ii) Bill very generously offers to give Anna a few of his autographs, so that they have the same number each.

How many will he give her?

Answer: .... (2)

13. (i) Bob had 24 marbles, but lost 9 of them.

How many did he then have?

Answer: .... (1)

(ii) Flora found 14 flowers and Freddy found 44 flowers.

How many flowers did Flora and Freddy find altogether?

Answer: .... (2)

PROBLEMS A

14. (i) Samantha ate four snails.

Sergei likes snails even more than Samantha and ate twice as many as Samantha.

(a) How many snails did Sergei eat?

Answer: .... (1)

(b) How many more snails did Sergei eat than Samantha?

Answer: .... (2)

(ii) Basil shared his 15 sweets equally between his three friends.
How many did each receive?

Answer: .... (1)

(iii) Wendy has 35 teddy bears and Brian has 19 fewer than Wendy.
How many do they have altogether?

Answer: .... (2)

(iv) Miss Pringle shared 26 sweets out as best she could between the eight pupils in her class.
How many sweets were left over?

Answer: .... (2)

15. A bucket holds six litres of water.

Five buckets of water are emptied into a bath.

Circle the calculation below which shows how you could work out how many litres of water are in the bath.

$5 + 6$ $\qquad$ $5 - 6$ $\qquad$ $5 + 5$ $\qquad$ $30 \div 6$

5×6 $\qquad$ $30 - 6$ $\qquad$ $11 - 6$ $\qquad$ $6 - 5$ $\qquad$ (2)

January 93 Q6

114

B **Reasoning about numbers or shapes:** working out numbers or shapes; number puzzles; making general statements

1. The sum of two numbers is 132

    One of the numbers is 57

    What is the other number?

    Answer: .... (2)

    January 98 Q1

2. (i) Bernard has three coins in his pocket.

        He has a total of 45 pence.

        What are the coins?

        Answer: .... (2)

    (ii) He buys a chocolate bar costing 29 pence, handing over two coins.

        He puts the change in his pocket.

        (a) How much money does he have left?

            Answer: .... pence (1)

        (b) He still has three coins!

            What are they?

            Answer: .... (1)

PROBLEMS B

3. There were 543 sweets in a jar.

   Jane guessed that the jar held 485 sweets and Mark thought that the jar held 629 sweets.

   (i) How far out was Jane's guess?

   Answer: .... (2)

   (ii) Whose guess was closest to the correct number of sweets in the jar?

   Answer: .... (2)

   January 97 Q6

4. Which is less money, 65p or $\frac{1}{2}$ of £1.50?

   Answer: .... (2)

   January 90 Q7

5. (i) Martin has these coins:

       10p   20p   1p   50p   50p   5p   2p   1p   2p   50p

   How much does he have altogether?

   Answer: £ .... (2)

   (ii) Amanda has these coins:

       20p   20p   1p   20p   10p   2p   2p   10p   1p   2p

   Draw circles round the coins she could use to pay **exactly** for something which costs 77p. (2)

6. Put a decimal point in the answer below to make it correct.

   $$3.2 \times 6.5 = 2\ 0\ 8$$

   Answer: ....2 . 0 . 8.............. (2)

   November 92 Q9

116

7. (i) What is a $\frac{1}{3}$ of a $\frac{1}{2}$ of 240?

Answer: .... (2)

(ii) A $\frac{1}{4}$ of a $\frac{1}{3}$ of a number is 12
     What is the number?

Answer: .... (2)

PROBLEMS B

8. The product of two whole numbers is 437
    What are the numbers?

Answer: .... (2)

9. The sum of two numbers is 120 and their product is 3599
    What are the numbers?

Answer: .... (2)

10. The product of three numbers is 30 and their sum is 10
    What are the numbers?

Answer: .... (2)

11.   Which is the **smallest** number which can be divided by both 30 and 42?

Answer: .... (3)

12.   Alice is thinking of a number.
      She multiplies it by 5 and then subtracts 4
      The result is 41
      What is her number?

B
PROBLEMS

Answer: .... (2)

13.   Kyle is thinking of a number.
      He multiplies it by 4 and then subtracts the result from 40
      The result is Kyle's number!
      What is it?

Answer: .... (2)

14.   Emily thinks of a number.
      She squares it and then adds her original number.
      The result is 56
      What is Emily's number?

Answer: .... (3)

15. The sum of three consecutive numbers is 66

    What is the product of the numbers?

    Answer: .... (3)

16. Clare has saved £3.75 in five-pence coins.

    How many coins does she have?

    Answer: .... (2)

17. Daniel has a special case which, when full, will hold nine of each of the following coins *(assume they are all the same thickness!)*:

    £1, 10p, 1p

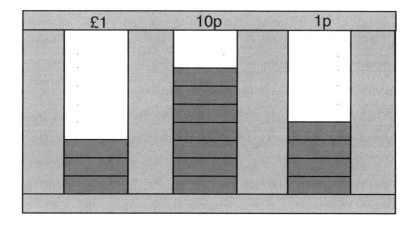

    (i) What is the value of the coins when the case is full?

    Answer: £ .... (1)

    (ii) What is the value of the coins in the case now?

    Answer: £ .... (1)

    (iii) What is the value of the coins which Daniel must put into the case in order to fill it?

    Answer: £ .... (2)

119

18. Steven has thought of a number and has given these clues.

The number is:

- 1 more than a square number
- larger than 10
- less than 100
- a multiple of 5

Find as many possibilities as you can for Steven's number.

Answer: .... (3)

19. Ruth has thought of a number and has given these clues.

The number is:

- smaller than 100
- one more than a multiple of 6
- the sum of the digits is 7

Find as many possibilities as you can for Ruth's number.

Answer: .... (3)

20. Lola has thought of two numbers

- their product is 48
- the difference between them is 8

What is the sum of Lola's numbers?

Answer: .... (3)

21. Here is part of a multiplication table.

×	2	4	6	8
2	4	8	12	16
3	6	12	18	24
4	8	16	24	32
5	10	20	30	40

(i) Which factors of 12 are shown in the table?

Answer: .... (2)

(ii) None of the numbers shown within the table is a prime number.
Give a reason why.

Answer: ....

....

.... (2)

(iii) Look at the pattern of numbers in the columns 4 and 8

(a) In which way does column 8 differ from column 4?

Answer: ....

....

.... (1)

(b) Why is this?

Answer: ....

....

.... (1)

Specimen 94 Q12

PROBLEMS B

22. Here are some multiplication wheels:

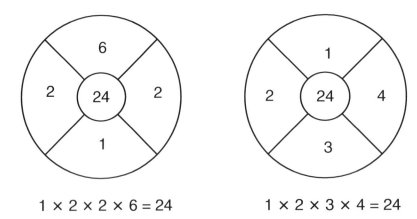

$1 \times 2 \times 2 \times 6 = 24$ $1 \times 2 \times 3 \times 4 = 24$

(i) Put a number in this wheel so that the answer in the centre is 24

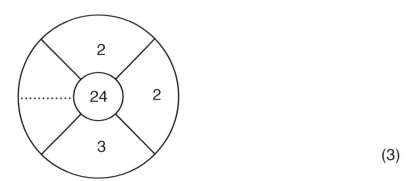

(3)

(ii) In the next two wheels the answers are missing.

Work out each answer and put it in the middle of the wheel.

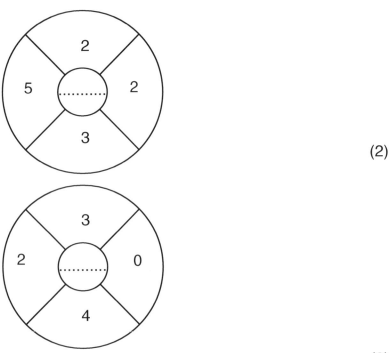

(2)

(2)

(iii)   Here are some wheels with missing numbers. Complete them.

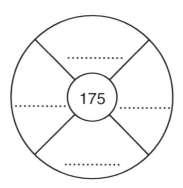

(3)

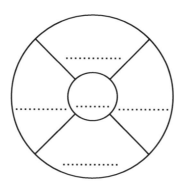

(3)

(iv)   Make up a multiplication wheel of your own, using the diagram below.

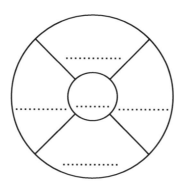

(4)

January 96 Q18

23. Using the number 2 three times, I can make many number sentences.

Example:

$$2 + 2 + 2 = 6$$
$$2 + 2 - 2 = 2$$
$$2 \times 2 \times 2 = 8$$
$$(2 \div 2) + 2 = 3$$

Using the number **3** three times, make as many number sentences as you can.

(6)

November 06 Q18

24. 144 oranges have to be packed in a rectangular box in six equal layers.

   (i) How many oranges are in each layer?

   Answer: .... (2)

   Each layer could be arranged in two rows of 12 oranges as shown in the diagram.

   O O O O O O O O O O O O
   O O O O O O O O O O O O

   (ii) Draw two more possible arrangements for each layer of oranges.

   (4)

   (iii) Investigate the possible packing arrangement if the 144 oranges were packed in four layers.

   (Your answers may either be written or drawn.)

   (7)

25. Look carefully at the calculation below.

To work out 16 × 21 we could use a doubling method like the ancient Egyptians.

$$1 \times 21 = 21$$
$$2 \times 21 = 42$$
$$4 \times 21 = 84$$
$$8 \times 21 = 168$$
$$16 \times 21 = 336$$

(i) Use the information above to work out

(a) 64 × 21

Answer: .... (3)

(b) 320 × 21

Answer: .... (3)

(c) 19 × 21

Answer: .... (4)

(ii) Using the doubling method and setting out the calculations as above, make up at least two more multiplications.

Example: 16 × 17 and 17 × 17

(4)

January 93 Q17

26.

0.2 $\qquad$ $\frac{4}{4}$ $\qquad$ $\frac{3}{15}$ $\qquad$ 0.25

$\frac{12}{15}$ $\qquad$ $\frac{1}{2}$ $\qquad$ $\frac{12}{16}$ $\qquad$ $\frac{8}{12}$

0.5 $\qquad$ $\frac{16}{20}$

$\frac{4}{20}$ $\qquad$ $\frac{2}{8}$ $\qquad$ $\frac{3}{12}$

$\frac{2}{4}$ $\qquad$ $\frac{3}{3}$

$\frac{4}{5}$ $\qquad$ $\frac{1}{1}$ $\qquad$ $\frac{4}{8}$

0.8 $\qquad$ $\frac{3}{6}$ $\qquad$ 0.75

$\frac{1}{4}$ $\qquad$ $\frac{2}{2}$

$\frac{9}{10}$ $\qquad$ $\frac{1}{5}$

Use the fractions and decimal fractions to make sets of numbers which belong together. List each set and give your reason for putting them together. You can use each fraction more than once and you can include fractions not given here.

See how many connections you can find.

....

....

....

....

....

....

....

....

....

....

.... (15)

January 91 Q21

27. The abacus pictures below show the numbers 21 and 120

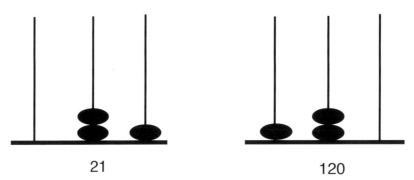

21   120

21 and 120 are multiples of 3

They are each shown using three beads on the abacus.

(i) On the abacus pictures below, draw three beads on each abacus to show all the other multiples of 3 which can be made using only three beads. Write the number shown under each picture.

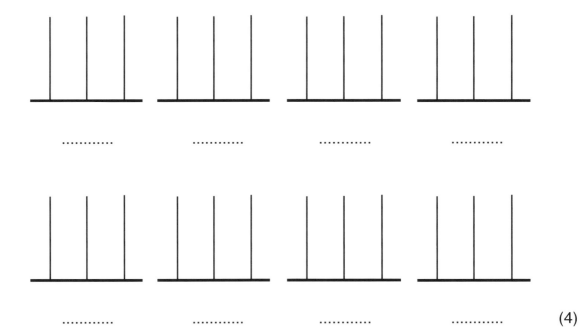

....

....   (4)

(ii) Now use the abacus pictures below to show which multiples of 4 can be made using only three beads; again, write the number below each abacus.

....   (2)

(iii)   In the same way, draw the multiples of 6 which can be shown using only three beads.

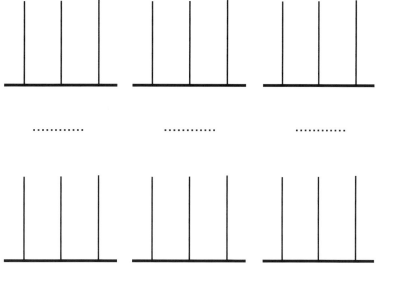

....

....   (3)

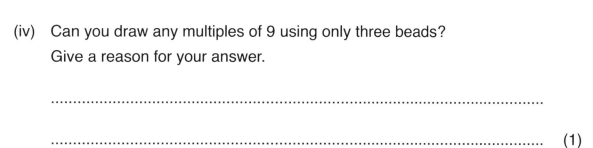

(iv)   Can you draw any multiples of 9 using only three beads?
Give a reason for your answer.

....

....   (1)

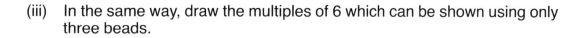

November 92 Q20

28.   Rearrange 3, 2, 6, 8 to make as many four-digit numbers as you can.
Example: 2638

(11)

January 92 Q18

29. Kiloran numbers have a digit sum of 8

　　　26 is a Kiloran number because　　　　$2 + 6 = 8$

　　　107 is a Kiloran number because　　　$1 + 0 + 7 = 8$

(i) List the Kiloran numbers less than 100, in order of increasing size.

Answer: 8, 17, ...

.... (4)

(ii) List the Kiloran numbers between 100 and 200, in order of increasing size.

Answer: ....

.... (3)

(iii) List the Kiloran numbers between 200 and 300, in order of increasing size.

Answer: ....

.... (2)

(iv) Without listing them, how many Kiloran numbers are there between 300 and 400?

Answer: .... (1)

(v) How many Kiloran numbers are there less than 1000?

Answer: .... (3)

30. Alexander numbers are

      • 1 more than a multiple of 7

      • 1 less than a multiple of 3

(i)   Find four numbers less than 80 which satisfy these conditions.

Answer: .... (4)

(ii) Look for a pattern in these numbers and use your pattern to find one more Alexander number less than 100

Answer: .... (1)

(iii) List the Alexander numbers between 100 and 200

Answer: .... (5)

(iv) Describe any interesting discoveries you have made with these numbers.

Answer: ....

....

.... (2)

31. Write one of the numbers 11, 12, 13, 14, 15, 16, 17, 18, 19 in each of the circles below so that

> 11, 19, 12 are somewhere in the top row
>
> 18, 14, 16 are somewhere in the bottom row
>
> 16, 13, 11, 15, 18, 19 are **not** in the left-hand column
>
> 15, 16, 12, 17, 14, 11 are **not** in the right-hand column.

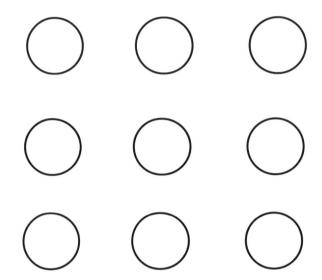

Use the space below to try out your ideas.

(9)

January 92 Q11

32. A pentomino is made from 5 squares. Here are five examples.

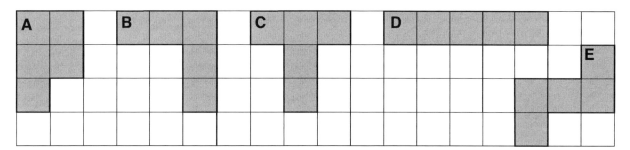

(i) Give the letters of the pentominoes above which have

    (a)   line symmetry   Answer: ....   (2)

    (b)   rotational symmetry.   Answer: ....   (2)

(ii) Give the letters of the pentominoes which can be folded to make an open box like this:

                                  Answer: ....   (2)

(iii) On the grid below, draw as many other different pentominoes as you can.

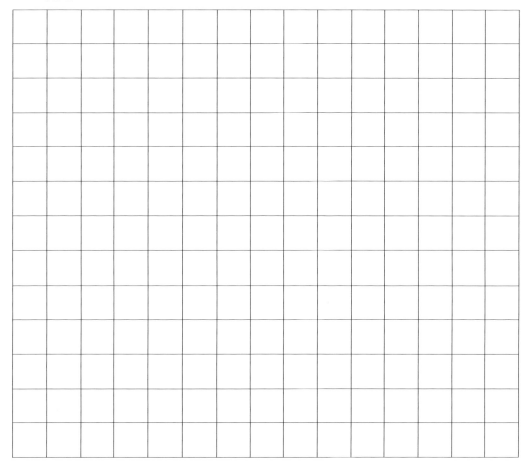

(4)

January 95 Q19

33. (i) Tim draws rectangles whose sides are whole numbers of centimetres. On the grid, two of his rectangles are drawn, each with a perimeter of 12 cm.

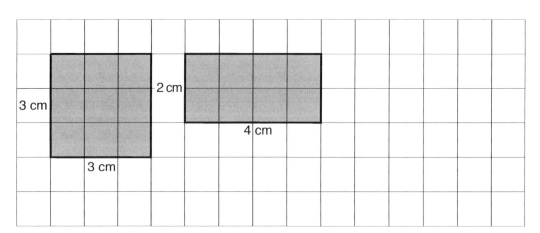

(a) On the grid, draw another rectangle with the same perimeter. (2)

(b) Put a tick inside the rectangle which has the greatest area. (1)

(ii) On this grid, Tim has drawn one rectangle with a perimeter of 20 cm.

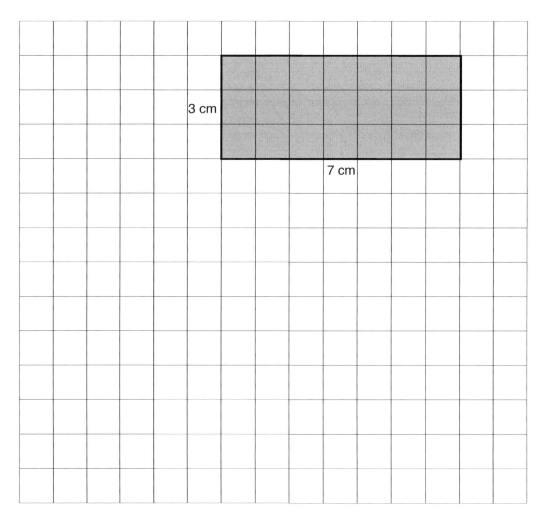

(a) On the grid, draw four other rectangles with a perimeter of 20 cm. (4)

(b) Put a tick inside the rectangle with the greatest area. (1)

(iii) Tim's father is building a rectangular patio.
He makes the perimeter of his patio 40 metres.

(a) What is the largest area of patio he can have?

Answer: .... m^2 (3)

(b) Explain how you decided what your answer would be.

Answer: ....

....

.... (2)

January 98 Q15

34. On the dotted grid, the distance between the dots is 1 cm. Making sure that the corners are on the dots, draw as many different shapes as you can with an area of 6 cm². *(One has been drawn for you.)*

136

(15)

November 91 Q20

35. (i) Draw in all the lines of symmetry of the shape shown on the grid below.

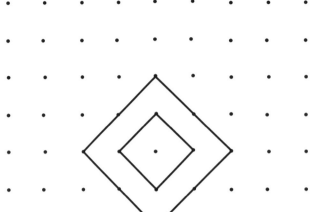

(2)

(ii) Draw some more designs using two different-sized squares, so that your designs have one line of symmetry only.

Show clearly the line of symmetry in each case.

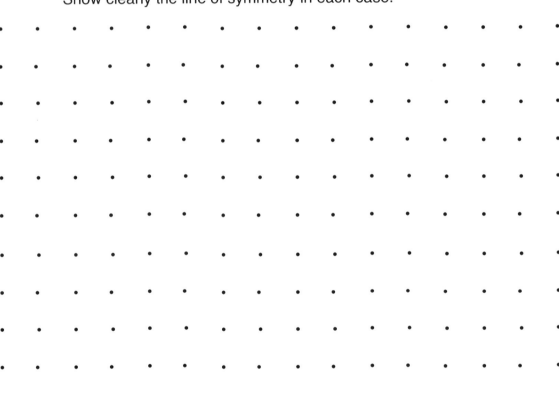

(6)

January 90 Q19

36. Here are four equilateral triangles drawn on an isometric dotted grid.

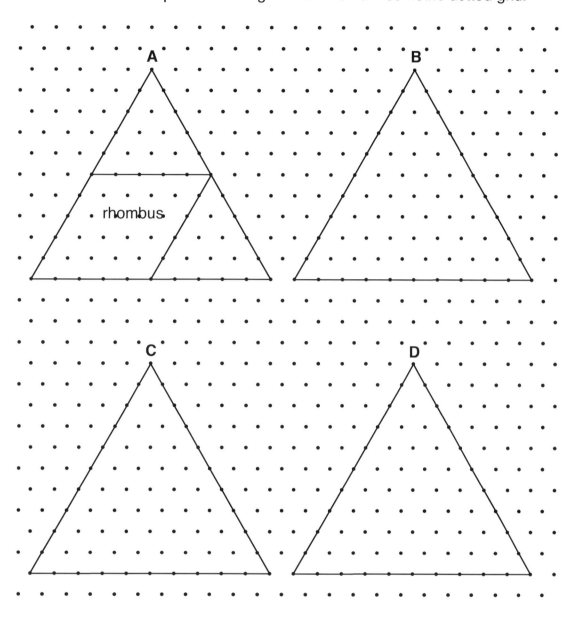

Triangle **A** has been cut to form two congruent equilateral triangles and a rhombus.

(i) Draw lines on triangle **B** to cut it into two similar equilateral triangles and a parallelogram. (2)

(ii) Draw lines on triangle **C** to cut it into two different isosceles trapeziums and one equilateral triangle. (2)

(iii) Draw lines on triangle **D** to cut it into three congruent equilateral triangles and a hexagon. (2)

37. (i) The shapes **A**, **B** and **C** have been made by joining together two congruent shapes like this one.

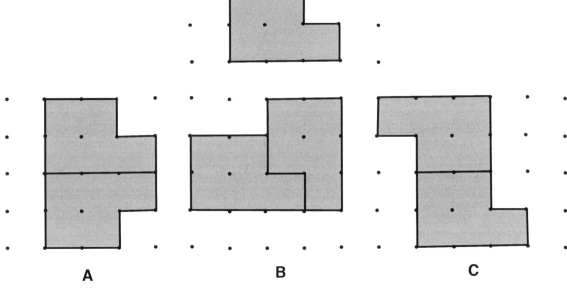

| A | B | C |

(a) Which shape has reflection symmetry?

Answer: .... (1)

(b) Which shape has rotation symmetry?

Answer: .... (1)

(c) Which shape has no symmetry?

Answer: .... (1)

(ii) On the dotted grid below, using the same simple piece, draw your own shapes, **D** with reflection symmetry and **E** with rotation symmetry.

| D | E |

(4)

38. In a pattern, hexagons are laid side by side, as shown.

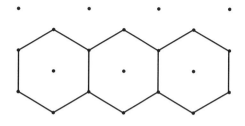

(i) Complete the table.

number of hexagons	1	2	3	4	5	6
number of outside edges	6	10				

(4)

(ii) Complete the statement.

To find the number of outside edges, first ....

the number of hexagons by .... and then

.... (3)

(iii) How many outside edges would there be if 100 hexagons were placed side by side?

Answer: .... (2)

January 99 Q16

141

39. Here are some patterns of triangles made up of matchsticks.

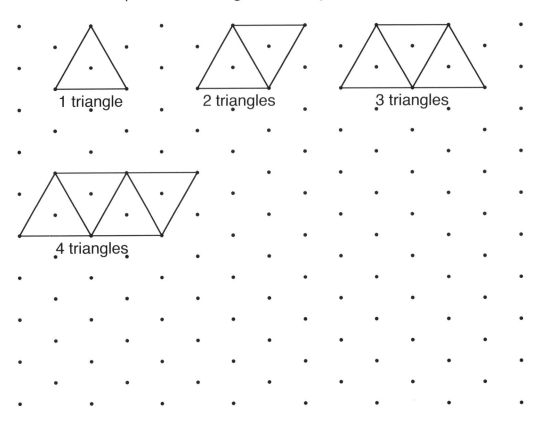

1 triangle   2 triangles   3 triangles

4 triangles

(i) Complete the following table.

(You may draw more patterns of triangles if you wish.)

number of triangles in a pattern	number of matchsticks
1	3
2	5
3	....
4	....
5	....
6	....

(4)

January 97 Q16

142

(ii) How many matchsticks are needed to make a pattern of

    (a)   12 triangles

Answer: .... (2)

    (b)   100 triangles?

Answer: .... (2)

(iii) What is the greatest number of triangles in a pattern which can be made from

    (a)   19 matchsticks

Answer: .... (2)

    (b)   41 matchsticks

Answer: .... (2)

    (c)   100 matchsticks?

Answer: .... (2)

40. Here are some squares drawn on a centimetre square grid. The points in the squares where the grid lines cross have been marked with dots.

The table below has been filled in for square **A**.

square	A	B	C	D	E
length of side in cm	1	2	....	....	....
perimeter in cm	4	....	....	....	....
area in cm²	1	....	....	....	....
number of dots	0	1	....	....	....

(i) (a) Complete the table for square **B** and square **C**. (3)

(b) On the grid, draw square **D** with sides 4 cm long. Mark in it the dots. (2)

(c) Complete the table for square **D**. (2)

(d) In the same way draw square **E** with sides 5 cm long and complete the table for **E**. (3)

144

(ii) Look at the number patterns in the table.

Using these patterns, work out for a square with sides 13 cm long

(a) its perimeter

Answer: .... cm   (2)

(b) its area

Answer: .... cm^2 (2)

(c) the number of dots inside it.

Answer: ....   (2)

November 96 Q16

145

41. Look at these squares drawn on dotted paper.

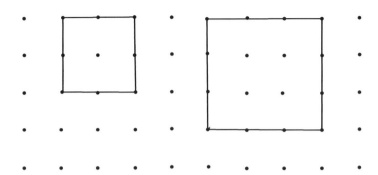

The table below is filled in for the first two squares.

(i) On the dotted paper opposite, draw squares with sides of 4 cm, 5 cm, 6 cm, 7 cm and 8 cm. (2)

length of side of square in cm	2	3	4	5	6	7	8
perimeter of square in cm	8	12	....	....	....	....	....
area of square in cm²	4	9	....	....	....	....	....
number of dots on perimeter	8	12	....	....	....	....	....
number of dots inside	1	4	....	....	....	....	....

(ii) Complete the table. (3)

(iii) (a) What pattern do you notice in the row of numbers for the perimeter of a square?

Answer: ....

.... (2)

(b) What pattern do you notice in the row of numbers for the area of a square?

Answer: ....

.... (2)

(iv) Use the patterns you have found to help you fill in these answers.

(a) A square with sides of 12 cm will have .... dots on the

perimeter and .... dots inside it. (2)

(b) A square with sides of 25 cm will have .... dots on the

perimeter and .... dots inside it. (2)

146

November 93 Q19

147

42. Look at these patterns:

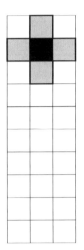 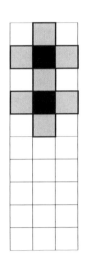 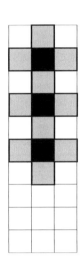 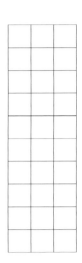

1 black tile   2 black tiles   3 black tiles
4 grey tiles   7 grey tiles   10 grey tiles

(i)   Draw the next pattern.   (1)

(ii) Complete this table for the number of tiles.

number of black tiles	number of grey tiles
1	4
2	7
3	10
4	....
5	....

(2)

148

(iii) How many grey tiles will be needed when there are

    (a)   six black tiles

Answer: ....   (1)

    (b)   ten black tiles?

PROBLEMS
B

Answer: ....   (2)

(iv) Describe a rule for working out the number of grey tiles needed when you are told the number of black tiles.

Answer: ....

....

....   (2)

(v) Use your rule to find how many grey tiles will be needed when there are 1000 black tiles.

Answer: ....   (2)

November 98 Q13

43. The cubes below have been arranged to form a double staircase.

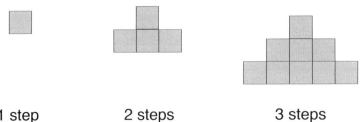

1 step   2 steps   3 steps
1 cube   4 cubes   9 cubes

(i) In the space below, draw the next two staircases and fill in the number of cubes.

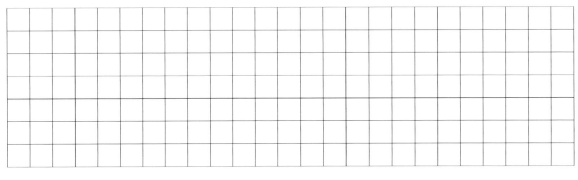

4 steps   5 steps

.... cubes   .... cubes   (6)

(ii) How many cubes would you need to make a 20-step double staircase?

Answer: .... (3)

(iii) How many steps would a double staircase which needs 64 cubes have?

Answer: .... (3)

November 90 Q22

C **'Real life' mathematics:** solving problems involving numbers in context; real life, money, measures

1. A baseball cap costs £5.20

   How much do four caps cost?

   Answer: £ .... (2)

November 95 Q1

2. Mary has saved £4.76 for a toy costing £10.15

   How much more money does she need?

   Answer: £ .... (2)

January 95 Q1

3. Patricia has £5.20 and Peter has £3.85

   How much more money does Patricia have than Peter?

   Answer: £ .... (2)

January 91 Q4

4. John saves $\frac{1}{4}$ of his pocket money each week towards a dictionary which costs £3.60

   He gets 80p pocket money each week.

   For how many weeks must he save?

   Answer: .... (3)

November 90 Q15

5. At a charity day, Year 6 raised these amounts of money:

           £11.94   £26.55   £2.87   £102.63

How much money did they raise altogether?

Answer: £ .... (2)

November 97 Q2

6. Susan was given some money for her birthday.

She spent £6.99 on a book and £1.99 on a pen.

  (i) How much did she spend?

Answer: £ .... (3)

She had £1.52 left.

  (ii) How much was she given?

Answer: £ .... (2)

January 96 Q2

7. Mr Brown buys five pints of milk costing 28 pence per pint, two loaves of bread costing 48 pence each and $\frac{1}{2}$ kg of tomatoes costing £1.30 per kg. How much does he spend altogether?

Answer: £ .... (2)

November 90 Q13

8. Suzie bought three sheets of card at 35p each sheet, two felt-tip pens costing
    49p each, a tube of glue at 62p and some clear plastic.

    Suzie received £2.08 change from £5

    How much did she pay for the plastic?

    Answer: .... pence   (6)

    January 91 Q16

9. A packet of sweets costs 18 pence.

    How much would 20 packets of these sweets cost?

    Answer: £ ....   (2)

    November 90 Q4

PROBLEMS
C

10. There are 24 children in a class.

    Each of them is given seven exercise books for the term.

    How many books are needed for the class?

    Answer: ....   (2)

    November 96 Q6

11. Ben is given £8

    He buys a book for £6.95

    How much money has he left?

    Answer: £ ....   (2)

    November 97 Q1

12. (i) I have £10

    What is the largest number of stickers I can buy if each sticker costs 9p?

    Answer: .... (3)

    (ii) How much change will I receive?

    Answer: .... pence (2)

    January 97 Q4

13. Grandma gave Mary, Jane, Joe and Paul £18 to share equally.
    How much did they each receive?

    Answer: £ .... (2)

    January 99 Q4

14. Six pencils cost £2.76
    What is the cost, in pence, of each pencil?

    Answer: .... pence (2)

    November 97 Q4

154

15. Sue bought a sweater in a sale for £7.35
    It had been reduced from £10
    How much less than £10 did Sue pay?

    Answer: £ .... (3)

January 90 Q8

16. At Maythorpe School there are 1002 pupils altogether.
    On the first Monday of a 'flu epidemic 289 children were absent.
    How many pupils attended on that day?

    Answer: .... (2)

January 91 Q18

17. (i)   A box holds 24 pencils.
         How many pencils are there in 16 boxes?

         Answer: .... (3)

    (ii) The school has 1290 pens.
          How many pen packets can be filled if each packet holds 15 pens?

          Answer: .... (2)

January 99 Q5

18. (i) Work out the cost of this shopping.

(a) 7 oranges at 28p each

Answer: £ .... (2)

(b) 9 grapefruit at 3 for 65p

Answer: £ .... (2)

(c) 500 g of tomatoes at £1.36 per kg

Answer: £ .... (2)

(d) $1\frac{1}{4}$ kg of leeks at 56p per kg

Answer: £ .... (2)

(e) 750 g of peanuts at £2.40 per kg

Answer: £ .... (2)

(ii) There is a special offer at the shop on a large bag of potatoes.

20 kg for only
£4.25

1 kg of potatoes normally costs 24p.

How much would I save if I bought the special offer 20 kg bag instead of 20 kg at the usual price?

Answer: .... pence (3)

January 95 Q11

PROBLEMS

C

19. Work out the prices I would pay for this shopping.

   (i)   5 kiwi fruit at 17p each

                                               Answer: .... pence (1)

   (ii)   3 pounds of carrots at 36p per pound

      Answer: £ .... (1)

   (iii)   6 eggs at £1.10 per dozen

      Answer: .... pence (2)

   (iv) $1\frac{1}{4}$ pounds of apples at 48p per pound

      Answer: .... pence (2)

   (v)   12 oranges at 3 for 45p

      Answer: £ .... (2)

   (vi)   500 g of butter at 65p for 250 g

      Answer: £ .... (2)

November 92 Q13

20. The cost of a week's shopping for three people is shown in this table:

	Mr Roberts	Miss Smith	Mrs Barnet
groceries	£22.50	£18.75	£15.05
bread	£ 1.95	£ 0.86	£ 3.67
meat	£ 7.80	£ 4.28	£12.95

   (i)   Who spends most on a week's shopping?

      Answer: .... (5)

   (ii)   How much change does Miss Smith have from £30?

      Answer: £ .... (3)

   (iii)   How much do the three people spend altogether?

      Answer: £ .... (3)

January 90 Q12

PROBLEMS
C

21. Find the cost of Mrs Brown's shopping from the prices shown.

(i) | potatoes 39p per kg |

What is the cost of 6 kg of potatoes?

Answer: £ .... (2)

(ii) | 4 oranges for 72p |

What is the cost of 12 oranges?

Answer: £ .... (2)

(iii) | apples £1.30 per kg |

What is the cost of $2\frac{1}{2}$ kg of apples?

Answer: £ .... (3)

Mrs Brown needs to buy onions.
There are two kinds.
For each, write the cost of 1 kg.

(iv) | 2 kg for £1.36 |

What would 1 kg cost?

Answer: .... pence (1)

(v) | 250 g for 18p |

What would 1 kg cost?

Answer: .... pence (2)

November 97 Q7

158

22. Uncle Harry gives Mary, Fred and Tim £15.24 to share equally.
     How much do they each get?

                              Answer: £ ....   (3)

November 96 Q5

23. Six pens cost £1.08
     How much does each pen cost?

                              Answer: .... pence   (2)

November 90 Q3

24. In my pocket, I have a 1p coin, a 10p coin and a 50p coin.
     How many sweets can I buy if each sweet costs 9p?

                              Answer: ....   (2)

November 92 Q3

25. How many ten-pence pieces are there in £87.50?

                              Answer: ....   (2)

January 92 Q6

26. Belinda bought two sweets costing 17p each and three costing 15p each.
     How much change did she have from £1?

                              Answer: .... pence   (3)

November 93 Q1

PROBLEMS
C

27. The Jones family went into a café.

The table shows what they ordered.

		cost, in £
3 cans of cola at 63 pence each		£1.89
2 cups of tea at 54 pence each		.......:.....
5 buns at 32 pence each		.......:.....
	total cost	.......:.....

(i) Complete the table. (3)

(ii) Mr Jones paid with a £10 note.

How much change did he get?

Answer: £ .... (2)

November 98 Q3f(a)

28. I buy three pencils costing 45p each.

How much change do I get from £2?

Answer: .... pence (2)

November 92 Q2

29. Jane bought six identical pencil cases to give to her friends.

She paid £5.94 for them altogether.

What was the cost of each pencil case?

Answer: .... pence (2)

January 95 Q4

30.   Mary buys eight packets of sweets.

Each packet contains 25 sweets.

(i)   How many sweets does she have altogether?

Answer: .... (2)

She then shares all these sweets equally between herself and the nine friends who come to her birthday party.

(ii)   How many sweets does each person receive?

Answer: .... (2)

January 96 Q7

31.   A minibus takes 17 people.

(i)   How many people would three minibuses take?

Answer: .... (1)

Mrs Jennings arranges a theatre trip for 74 people.

(ii)   How many minibuses does she need?

Answer: .... (2)

January 98 Q8

PROBLEMS
C

32. A man is travelling with his son by bus.

He pays a total of £1.35

The man pays full fare and his son pays half.

What are the father's fare and son's fare for the journey?

Answer: father .... pence

son .... pence   (4)

November 95 Q8

33. (i) Complete the following bill.

5 lb	apples at	22p per lb	£	(2)
12	oranges at	.... p each	£1.44	(2)
....	grapefruit at	24p each	£1.20	(2)
		total	£	(2)

(ii) How much change should you receive from a £5 note?

Answer: £ ....   (2)

November 94 Q5

34. How many bars of chocolate costing 25p each can be bought for £5?

Answer: ....   (3)

January 90 Q1

35. 12 chocolate bars cost £1.68

    What is the cost of each bar?

    Answer: .... pence   (2)

    November 92 Q4

36. A mug costs £1.35

    What is the cost of a set of six mugs?

    Answer: £ ....   (2)

    February 94 Q3

37. Four pairs of socks cost £11.80

    What is the cost of one pair?

    Answer: £ ....   (3)

    January 93 Q2

38. John paid for some food with a £5 note.

    He received £2.81 in change.

    How much did the food cost?

    Answer: £ ....   (2)

    January 92 Q1

39. Amy emptied out the contents of her purse.

    She had 1 penny, 2 two-pence coins, 5 five-pence coins, 10 ten-pence coins and 20 twenty-pence coins.

    How much did she have altogether?

    Answer: £ ....   (4)

PROBLEMS C

163

40. In the school shop, these are the prices of some things for sale:

> pencils 27p each
>
> stickers 8p each
>
> notebooks £1.50 each

Mrs Brown needs 99 stickers.

To save multiplying by 99, she works out the cost like this:

100 stickers cost 100 × 8p which is 800p, which is £8.00

She then takes away the cost of 1 sticker to find the cost of 99

£8.00 − 8p is £7.92

Use Mrs Brown's method to work out the cost of

(i) 99 pencils

Answer: £ .... (3)

(ii) 99 notebooks.

Answer: £ .... (3)

November 96 Q12

41. Mrs Jones has a dress shop.

She buys some dresses for £28.59 each.

She sells the dresses for £40 each.

(i) How much profit does she make on each dress?

Answer: £ .... (2)

At the end of the season she has one dress left.

She reduces its selling price by 30%

(ii) What reduction does she make on the price of the dress?

Answer: £ .... (3)

(iii) For this last dress, has Mrs Jones made a profit or a loss on the price she paid for it?

Answer: .... (1)

January 98 Q13(b)

42. (i) Mrs Jones bought a cardigan costing £40

   During the sale, the price was reduced by 10%

   (a) What would she have saved if she had bought the cardigan during the sale?

   Answer: £ .... (2)

   (b) What was the sale price of the cardigan?

   Answer: £ .... (2)

   (ii) The label on a blouse states:

55% polyester
35% cotton

   What is wrong with this label?

   Answer: ....

   .... (2)

   January 99 Q11(b)

166

43. A theatre outing is being planned.

Look at the seating plan below.

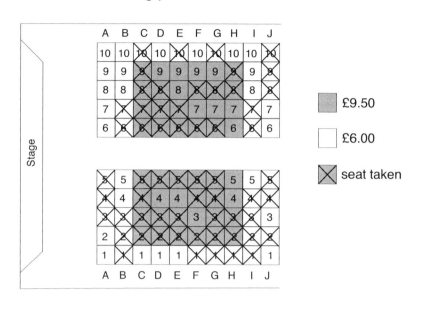

(i) 15 seats are needed, all at the same price.
At what price are there 15 seats available?

Answer: £ .... (2)

(ii) Calculate the total cost of the 15 tickets.

Answer: £ .... (2)

(iii) The total cost of the outing, including travel, tickets and 50p per person for a programme or a drink, comes to £131.25
Calculate each person's travel contribution.

Answer: £ .... (4)

(iv) Each seat can be identified by a letter and a number, such as A7.
Using the whole plan above, make a list from the available seats, so that all 15 people can sit next to at least one person in the group.

Answer: ....

.... (2)

January 92 Q16

167

44.

CAR PARK OPEN 08:00 – 20:00 CAR PARK CHARGES	
up to 1 hour	60p
1 to 2 hours	£1.10
2 to 3 hours	£1.50
3 to 4 hours	£1.80
4 to 6 hours	£2.00
6 to 8 hours	£2.50
over 8 hours	£3.00

(i)   Mr Brown parked from 13:25 to 14:20

How much did he have to pay?

Answer: .... pence   (1)

(ii)   Mrs Pringle parked from 13:05 to 16:00

For how long did Mrs Pringle park?

Answer: .... minutes   (2)

(iii)   Dr Clarke parked from 10:42 to 16:10

How much did he have to pay?

Answer: £ ....   (2)

(iv)   Miss Sefton parked at 11:00

She returned at 19:02

How much did she have to pay?

Answer: £ ....   (2)

(v)   What was the latest possible time she could have left the car park that day?

Answer: ....   (2)

January 93 Q9

168

45. 150 plastic ducks of different colours were sold for a charity duck race on a local river.

The ducks were identical, apart from their colour.

The chart shows the colours and the numbers of ducks sold.

yellow	50	pink	....
red	19	blue	16
white	....	green	15

The same number of pink ducks was sold as white ducks.

(i) Complete the table. (2)

(ii) The stall holder bought the ducks for 22p each and he sold them for 50p each.

He gave all the profit to charity.

What was the total profit made?

Answer: £ .... (3)

(iii) Which colour duck was most likely to win?

Answer: .... (1)

(iv) Tom bought three yellow ducks.

Jane bought one yellow, one pink and one white duck.

Tom said, 'I stand a better chance of winning because all my ducks are yellow.'

Is Tom's statement correct? Explain your answer.

Answer: ....

....

.... (2)

January 99 Q12

169

PROBLEMS
C

46. When building a fence 36 metres long, a man uses posts spaced four metres apart.

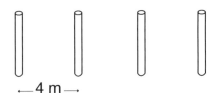

—4 m—

(i)   How many posts will he need?

Answer: .... (3)

He then joins these posts with slats, as in the diagram.

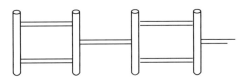

(ii)   How many slats will he need?

Answer: .... (2)

(iii)   What total length of wood will he need for the slats?

Answer: .... m (2)

January 99 Q15

47. From this list of quadrilaterals, choose the correct name for each box of the decision tree diagram.

parallelogram   **rectangle**   **rhombus**   **square**   **trapezium**

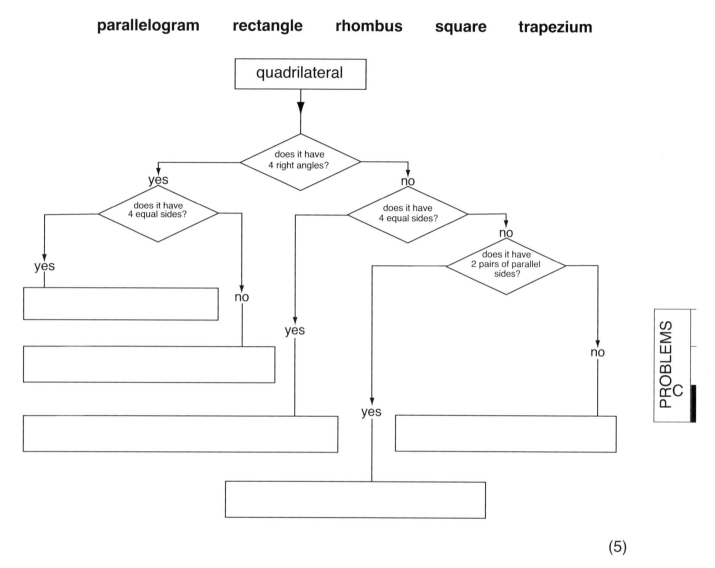

(5)

November 92 Q14

48. The table below gives some information about secondhand cars which are for sale.

Use the table to answer the questions.

name of owner	colour of car	number of doors	price
Miss Benn	green	two	£8 000
Mr Brown	black	four	£3 500
Mrs Felton	red	two	£10 900
Mr Harper	white	four	£11 350
Miss Park	silver	two	£2 750
Mrs Silver	green	four	£7 150

(i) Whose car has the lowest value?

Answer: .... (1)

(ii) Mrs Felton sells her car for the price in the table.

How much more money does she need to be able to buy Mr Harper's car?

Answer: £ .... (3)

(iii) A car dealer buys Mrs Silver's car and Miss Benn's car.

How much does he have left from £20 000?

Answer: £ .... (3)

(iv) Mr Brown sells his car for £3500

He has to give 50% of this to his sister.

How much does he give her?

Answer: £ .... (3)

January 93 Q14

172

49. The table shows how long six girls remained silent and the amount of money they raised during a sponsored charity silence.

	time	amount
Jane	1 h 30 min	£15
Mary	40 min	£10.25
Joanne	1 h 15 min	£3.75
Claire	1 h 20 min	£20
Lucy	1 h	£14
Sally	45 min	£22.50

(i)   What was the total amount raised?

Answer: £ .... (2)

(ii) What was the mean (average) amount raised by each girl?

Answer: £ .... (2)

(iii) What was the mean (average) length of time that each girl remained silent?

Answer: .... minutes (3)

(iv) How much money did Jane raise per hour?

Answer: £ .... (2)

Specimen 94 Q10

PROBLEMS
C

50. Five motorists used a car park.

PARKING	up to 2 hours:	50p
FEES	2–4 hours:	60p
	more than 4 hours:	£1

On the table, complete the times and fees charged.

car	entered car park	parking time	left car park	fee charged
FIESTA	09:00	3 h 10 min	....	.... p
METRO	09:01	..... h ..... min	11:05	.... p
ESCORT	....	5 h 10 min	14:15	£1
SAAB	09:08	..... h ..... min	10:10	.... p
PEUGEOT	....	1 h 50 min	11:00	50p

(8)

Specimen 94 Q16

51. A class is to make biscuits in a cookery lesson.

Here is the recipe each pupil uses to make 12 biscuits:

175 g plain flour

50 g cornflour

220 g butter

75 g icing sugar.

(i) There are 14 children in the class.

How many biscuits will they make altogether?

Answer: .... (2)

(ii)   How much plain flour will the class need for this lesson?

Answer: .... g   (2)

(iii) The teacher opens a three kilogram packet of flour.
       How many grams will be left at the end of the lesson?

Answer: .... g   (2)

(iv)   What is the total mass of ingredients used by each pupil?

Answer: .... g   (2)

(v)   The biscuits lose 10% of their mass when they are cooked.
       What will be the mass of one pupil's cooked biscuits?

Answer: .... g   (2)

(vi)   The cost of each pupil's ingredients is 48p.
       What is the cost of each biscuit?

Answer: .... pence   (1)

(vii) Six children sell all their biscuits for 6p each in aid of the school charity.
       How much money will they receive altogether?

Answer: £ ....   (2)

November 93 Q14

175

52. A classroom is 11 metres long and 7.5 metres wide.

    (i)   What is the area of the classroom floor?

                              Answer: .... m² (2)

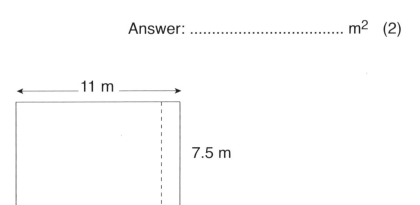

    A partition is erected across the back of the classroom, one metre from the back wall, as shown in the diagram by the dotted line.

    (ii) By how many square metres has the floor area been reduced?

                              Answer: .... m² (2)

    (iii) What is the new classroom floor area?

                              Answer: .... m² (2)

300 square tiles are laid on the new classroom floor as shown below.

10 m

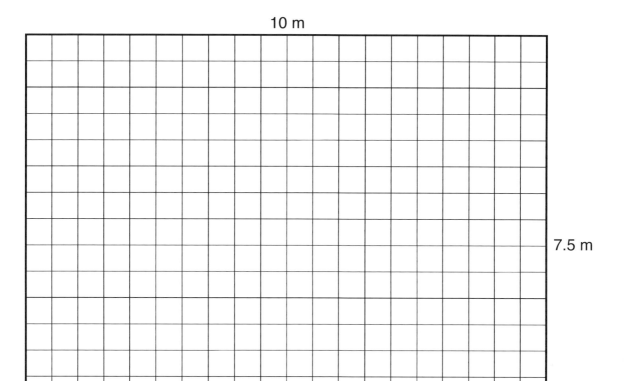

7.5 m

(iv)   What is the length of a side of a tile?

Answer: .... m   (2)

Some of the tiles are dark-coloured and some are light-coloured.

The pattern of tiling is shown below, starting with a five by five square (outlined here) in the top left-hand corner.

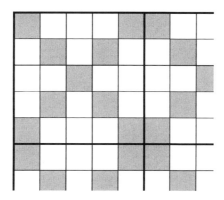

(v)   What fraction of the floor is covered with dark tiles?

Answer: ....   (2)

53. A plan of the school hall is shown below.

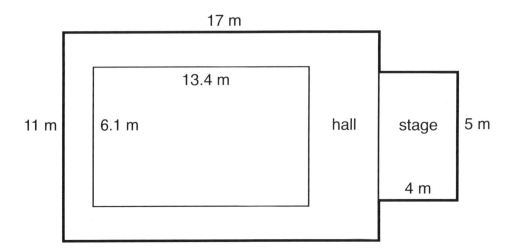

(i) What is the area of the stage?

Answer: .... m² (1)

(ii) What is the area of the floor of the hall?

Answer: .... m² (2)

A badminton court 13.4 m long and 6.1 m wide is marked on the floor as shown on the plan.

(iii) What is the perimeter of the court?

Answer: .... m (2)

The stage has special non-slip flooring which costs £9.95 per square metre.

(iv) What is its **approximate** cost?

Answer: £ .... (2)

The parents have raised £800 for stage lights.
These lights cost £199.95 each.

(v) How many stage lights can they afford?

Answer: .... (2)

November 93 Q15

54. The information on a caramel slice is

per 100 g	
protein	5 g
fat	21 g
carbohydrate	60 g

(i) What fraction of the slice is protein?

Answer: .... (2)

(ii) What percentage of the slice is carbohydrate?

Answer: .... % (1)

(iii) The caramel slice actually has a mass of 55 g.

What will be the mass of carbohydrate in the slice?

Answer: .... g (3)

(iv) One caramel slice costs 29 pence.

Amanda buys nine slices.

How much change will she receive from a £10 note?

Answer: £ .... (3)

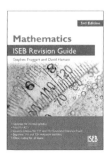
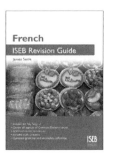
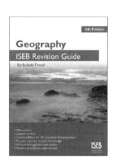

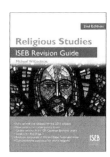
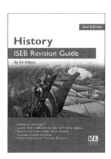

    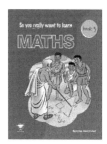
  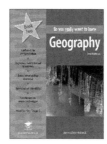  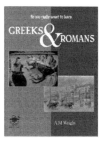